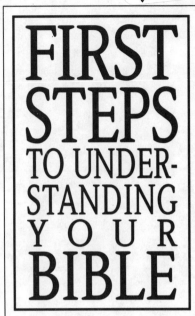

FIRST STEPS
TO UNDER-
STANDING
Y O U R
BIBLE

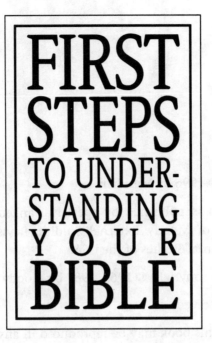

FIRST STEPS TO UNDER-STANDING YOUR BIBLE

PRESENTED TO

_____

_____

_____

FROM

_____

_____

MERIDIAN
PUBLICATIONS

M021X Paperback Study Edition
ISBN 156570-021-X

Cover design by Gayle Raymer
Book design by Blue Water Ink

A Meridian Publication

Printed in the United States of America

Contents

Preface

To begin to find the Christian life in all its fullness, we must first grasp all that is promised to us and required of us by God's Word and begin to apply it.

First Steps to Understanding Your Bible was initially developed and taught at Moody Bible Institute in Chicago. Since 1965 it has been part of a Bible correspondence course for the External Studies Division of Moody Bible Institute.

Now, for the first time, this incisive and insightful study is available for personal or group Bible study to help believers understand God's Word and come to enjoy the Christian life as God intended it.

—The Publisher

Introduction

"All scripture is given by inspiration of God," the King James Version of the Bible says. *First Steps to Understanding Your Bible* will guide you into a clear understanding of the Bible. Designed as a concise overview of biblical teaching, this book will teach you how to begin the journey of knowing God's Word.

This book and others in the *Christian Life Application* series provide study materials on the various aspects of living a full, rich Christian life. Meridian titles in addition to *First Steps to Understanding Your Bible* in the *Christian Life Application* series currently include:

First Steps to Discovering God

First Steps to Knowing God's Will

First Steps for New Christians

Additional titles in the *Christian Life Application* series are forthcoming.

Because these materials were initially used both as classroom and correspondence school texts, the style is that of a teacher—guiding, challenging, directing, stimulating, and raising questions as well as providing answers.

The content of this edition is taken from an adult credit course from the External Studies Division of Moody Bible

Institute. For information on how you might take this and other courses for credit, write for a free catalog to:

Moody External Studies
Moody Bible Institute
820 N. La Salle
Chicago, IL 60610

1

What We Are Told about the Bible

Various names are used for the Bible, such as *The Holy Bible, The Scriptures,* and *The Word of God.* The word *Bible* comes from a Greek word that originally meant "books," but which through a gradual change of usage came to be known in singular: "book." The title is remarkably apt; for this is, beyond question, *The Book.* The Bible is called "holy" because of its sacred character as coming from God. The term *scriptures* means "writings." This is the title most often used in the Bible itself, occurring about fifty times (including both the singular and the plural forms). Paul, in writing to Timothy, uses the expression, "the holy scriptures" (2 Timothy 3:15).

The Bible is made up of two parts, the Old Testament and the New Testament. The word *testament,* as used in this connection, means "covenant" or "agreement." The Old Testament has thirty-nine books and is the record of the covenant that God made with man about his salvation before Christ came into the world. The New Testament, containing twenty-seven books, is the covenant God made with man about salvation after Christ came.

THE BIBLE IS INSPIRED OF GOD

"All scripture is given by inspiration of God, and is profitable for doctrine, for reproof, for correction, for instruction in righteousness: that the man of God may be perfect, thoroughly furnished unto all good works" (2 Timothy 3:16–17).

1. Because God spoke it

David said, "The Spirit of the LORD spoke by me, And His word was on my tongue" (2 Samuel 23:2 NKJV). The Lord told Jeremiah, "Behold, I have put My words in your mouth" (Jeremiah 1:9 NKJV). The prophets said again and again, "Thus says the Lord GOD" (Ezekiel 5:5 NKJV).

In the New Testament Paul wrote to the Thessalonian church that his "exhortation did not come from error or uncleanness, nor was it in deceit" (1 Thessalonians 2:13).

2. Because God caused men to write it in his name

Some people maintain that the Bible only *contains* the

Word of God, thereby setting themselves up as judges to determine what in the Bible is inspired and what is not. On the contrary, the true statement of the case is: The Bible *is* the Word of God.

The Bible originated from God who caused consecrated men to write down exactly what he wanted written:

> For prophecy never came by the will of man, but holy men of God spoke as they were moved by the Holy Spirit (2 Peter 1:21 NKJV).

The word "moved" in this verse is used in Greek to describe the moving of a ship by the wind; thus, Bible writers were "borne along" by the Spirit when they wrote.

Since thoughts cannot be divorced from words; the very words of the original Scriptures were given by God, as Paul tells us in 1 Corinthians 2:13. This doctrine is called *verbal inspiration.* Sometimes the term *plenary inspiration* is used, to indicate that the whole Bible is God-breathed. The Bible asserts this to be a fact without telling us exactly how God did it. In some way, mysterious to us, God influenced the writers of Scripture to record his own Word, working through them in such a way that their personalities are evident. John did not write in the same style as Paul; yet that which each wrote is the Word of God.

THE BIBLE IS THE REVELATION OF GOD

Revelation is God's act of making known that which otherwise could never be known. Men always have sought to discover the truth concerning God and his relationship to the world, but the things of God cannot be found by ordinary human means:

But as it is written:
"Eye has not seen, nor ear heard,
Nor have entered into the heart of man
The things which God has prepared for those who
   love Him."
But God has revealed them to us through His Spirit
(1 Corinthians 2:9–10a NKJV).

The Bible is both a revelation from God and a revelation of God, for it comes from God and tells us about him. This revelation is twofold.

1. *God reveals himself in his written word*

But these are written that you may believe that Jesus is the Christ, the Son of God, and that believing you may have life in His name (John 20:31 NKJV).

And beginning at Moses and all the prophets, he expounded unto them in all the scriptures the things concerning himself (Luke 24:27 ; see also Luke 1:1–4; 24:44; John 5:39–47; Acts 1:1–2).

2. *God reveals himself in his Son,*
Jesus Christ, the Living Word

In the beginning was the Word, and the Word was with God, and the Word was God. . . . And the word was made [became, NASB] flesh, and dwelt among us (and we beheld his glory, the glory as of the only begotten of the Father), full of grace and truth (John 1:1, 14).

God, who at various times and in various ways spoke in time past to the fathers by the prophets, has in these last days spoken to us by His Son (Hebrews 1:1–2a).

THE BIBLE IS TRUSTWORTHY

Apart from the Bible there is no certainty. The Word of God is the only infallible rule of faith and practice:

Forever, O LORD, Your word is settled in heaven (Psalm 119:89 NKJV).

Someone has said, "If a man lies to me once, I wouldn't know when to trust him if he told me the truth a thousand times." The Bible does not lie to man even once. We can have confidence that what it says regarding spiritual things is true because what it says about geography and history is true.

An illustration of this concerns the last king of Babylon at the time of its fall to the Persians in 539 B.C. Historians said Nabonidus was king; the Bible said Belshazzar. Was the Bible wrong? No. Tablets have since been uncovered by archaeologists in Babylon showing that Belshazzar was co-ruler with his father Nabonidus. Here is an instance when an account in the Bible has been shown to be true.

THE BIBLE IS GOD'S MESSAGE TO MAN

Since the Bible is our guidebook, and since our conduct is to be governed in all things by what the Scriptures teach, let us see what particular things we should give attention to above all the rest. They are summarized in the following three statements.

1. *God's only plan of salvation*

The Scriptures teach what God has done and is doing for the salvation of mankind. Some people are trying to work for their salvation by various ways and means, but God tells us that we can know and experience salvation only through his Son.

> For I am not ashamed of the gospel of Christ, for it is the power of God to salvation for everyone who believes, for the Jew first and also for the Greek (Romans 1:16 NKJV).

> And that from childhood you have known the Holy Scriptures, which are able to make you wise for salvation through faith which is in Christ Jesus (2 Timothy 3:15).

2. *Man's responsibility to accept God's salvation*

The Scriptures teach what men must do to become partakers of this salvation: that is, they teach what men must do to be saved. Men might possibly know about the love and mercy of God without the Bible, but the way to be saved is found only in the Bible.

> So they said, "Believe on the Lord Jesus Christ, and you will be saved, you and your household" (Acts 16:31 NKJV).

> For God so loved the world that He gave His only begotten Son, that whoever believes in Him should not perish but have everlasting life (John 3:16 NKJV).

> As many as received him, to them gave he power to become the sons of God, even to them that believe on his name (John 1:12 NKJV).

Just as a person accepts a gift from a friend with no thought of paying for it, so men receive the gift of eternal life freely. One does not earn eternal life by his good life; it simply becomes his when he believes that Christ died and rose again for him.

3. *Man's condition in the life to come*

The Scriptures teach what the condition of man will be in the life to come; that is, how man will live and what he will do (Revelation 21:3–8). In every age men have tried earnestly to find out something about conditions in the life to come without the aid of the Bible. They have tried fortune-telling and they have tried talking with the dead. But the foolishness and sinfulness of such a course is seen in Isaiah 8:19 and Luke 16:29–31. In contrast to the doubts, uncertainty, and despair of men, the Bible gives us a true and sure message about the life to come.

We hold in our hands the most wonderful message of all time and of all eternity. It is indeed the Word of God; in it the God of heaven has told us about himself and about our relationship to him. What study could be more valuable than the study of the Bible? By God's grace we ought to be diligent in storing it up in our minds and hearts.

2

What the Bible Says about God

Look at the stars some night when the sky is clear. The Milky Way, stretching across the heavens, is a galaxy containing about 100 billion stars. Since scientists know of the existence of ten billion galaxies like ours, they estimate that there are about as many stars in the sky as there are grains of sand on all the seashores of the world! The psalmist says, "By the word of the LORD the heavens were made, . . . for he spoke, and it was done" (Psalm 33:6, 9 NKJV). This is the God revealed in the Bible. The Bible does not try to prove the existence of God; it reveals him in the following ways.

GOD IS A SPIRIT (John 4:24)

Most people find it difficult to think of reality apart from material things. All about us are things that we can see and touch. But God, who is the greatest reality of all, cannot be seen or touched because he is a Spirit. The Bible speaks of God (Colossians 1:15). From the words of the Lord Jesus in Luke 24:39, it is clear that a spirit does not have bodily form. No one has ever seen a pure spirit, that is, a spirit without some outward form.

The fact that God is a Spirit involves the additional fact that he is a personal Being who knows and thinks and acts—not some vague, impersonal force. It is this fact of personality that causes the Bible to say that man was made in the image of God.

IN HIS BEING GOD IS . . .

1. Infinite

God is different from every other spirit because he is infinite. Whatever other spirits there are have been created by him; and they are all finite or limited. God is not limited or confined in any way.

2. Eternal

"Eternal" means more than "endless." A thing may be endless once it has a beginning; but God had no beginning and he will have no end. This is the sense in which God is eternal—"Even from everlasting to everlasting, You *are* God" (Psalm 90:2 NKJV). Every other spirit had a beginning because God made it, but God himself was not made or caused by anyone or anything. He has eternal self-existence.

> "I am Alpha and Omega, the beginning and the ending, saith the Lord, which is, and which was, and which is to come, the Almighty" (Revelation 1:8).

3. Unchangeable

Because God is perfect, he could not possibly change. What he always has been he is now and always will be. Change is characteristic of finite beings and things. The infinite, eternal God is always the same, immutable in his absolute perfection. He says, "I am the LORD, I change not" (Malachi 3:6 ; see also Hebrews 13:8; James 1:17).

THE ATTRIBUTES OF GOD

The attributes of God are the qualities of his being that determine his activity, those things that are characteristic of God. There is no easy way to classify these attributes, although some students of the Bible divide them into the natural attributes and the moral attributes. His natural attributes are those that are true of God alone and cannot be passed on to any creature. His moral attributes are qualities that God has in absolute perfection, but which he can also give in a relative sense to his creatures, men and angels.

1. His natural attributes

a. *Omniscience.* God has a complete and perfect knowledge of all things, including all those things that are possible as well as all things which are actual in the past, present, and future. This perfect knowledge of all things is known as God's omniscience. God exercises this perfect knowledge in a perfect manner for his own glory and the good of his creation. This is infinite wisdom:

> O the depth of the riches both of the wisdom and knowledge of God! how unsearchable are his judgments, and his ways past finding out! (Romans 11:33).

> Such knowledge is too wonderful for me; it is high, I cannot attain unto it (Psalm 139:6 ; see also vv. 1–5).

b. *Omnipotence.* God is able to do anything that he wills to do. His power is unlimited; he is the "Almighty God" (Genesis 17:1). This attribute is called omnipotence. The God who created the universe out of nothing can do anything.

> "I am God, and there is none like me . . . saying I will do all my pleasure" (Isaiah 46:9–10).

Naturally God cannot do anything that would involve sin or absurdity for that would be out of harmony with his nature, but this is not a limitation of his power; it is instead an affirmation of it. When the Bible says that God "cannot lie" (Titus 1:2), it is not putting a limit upon his omnipotence. (See Psalm 62:11; Ephesians 3:20–21; Matthew 28:18.)

c. *Omnipresence.* God is present everywhere. We cannot understand this fully, and we must avoid thinking of God as if he were some kind of rare material substance stretching to every part of the universe and divisible into many parts. No, since God is an infinite Spirit, he is personally present everywhere. As someone has put it, "All of God is in every place." This attribute is called God's *omnipresence.* (See 1 Kings 8:27; Psalm 139:7–12.)

2. His moral attributes

a. *Holiness.* All through the Bible, both in the Old Testament and in the New, God is described as holy. For example, twenty-five times in the book of Isaiah alone God is called the "Holy One of Israel." The heavenly host praise him in these words:

> Holy, holy, holy, Lord God Almighty, which was, and is, and is to come (Revelation 4:8).

Holiness is difficult to define. Negatively it means that God is absolutely separate from all evil, from all that would defile. Positively it is the assertion of his absolute moral purity and rightness:

> God is light, and in him is no darkness at all (1 John 1:5).

b. *Justice.* This term is used interchangeably in the Scripture with the word "righteousness." Since God is perfectly holy in all he is, he naturally is perfectly right or just in all he does. He manifests his righteousness in his hatred of sin and his love of holiness.

> The LORD is righteous in her midst, He will do no unrighteousness. Every morning He brings His justice to light; He never fails, but the unjust knows no shame (Zephaniah 3:5 NKJV).

God's righteousness and holiness demand that he punish the sinner for his sin (Psalm 9:7–8; Acts 17:31; Revelation 6:10).

c. *Goodness.* Only God is absolutely good, as the Lord

Jesus reminded the rich young ruler (Matthew 19:17). This word may be thought by some to be synonymous with holiness, but it includes primarily the thought of God's benevolence, of the exercise of mercy or loving-kindness toward men.

> You are good, and do good; teach me Your statutes (Psalm 119:68 NKJV).

d. *Love.* Love is that delight in, and desire for, the welfare of his creatures that causes God to manifest himself in the person and work of his Son, the Lord Jesus Christ. So important is this attribute that the Bible says, "God is love" (1 John 4:8).

We must understand, however, that this love is in perfect harmony with his holiness and all his other attributes. God's love was especially manifest at the cross of Christ. (See John 3:16; Romans 5:8; 1 John 4:9–10.) Here God's holiness was satisfied, for the penalty of sin was paid, and at the same time his love was shown in his provision of forgiveness for all who believe.

e. *Truth.* We have already noted that God "cannot lie." He is true in all his ways. This attribute involves also God's faithfulness in fulfilling all his promises.

> A God of truth and without iniquity, just and right is he (Deuteronomy 32:4).

Let us remember that God's holiness, justice, goodness, love, and truth are just as infinite, eternal, and unchangeable as he is; for they are all qualities of his being.

❡

THE ONLY TRUE AND LIVING GOD

1. There is but one God

A little boy was once asked how he knew there was but one God, to which he replied, "Because there's room for only one—he fills heaven and earth." We have already seen that God is infinite; so the boy was right.

There is none other God but one (1 Corinthians 8:4).

Hear, O Israel: The LORD our God is one LORD (Deuteronomy 6:4; see also Isaiah 44:8; James 2:19; 1 Timothy 2:5).

2. This God is the living God

He is called "living" because he is the source of life. (See John 1:4; 5:26.) All life comes from God.

a. *Natural Life.* God created Adam a "living soul" (Genesis 2:7). The life that we enjoy comes from God. We should thank him for every breath that we draw. (See Acts 17:28; Colossians 1:17.)

b. *Spiritual Life.* Through the new birth the believer enters into spiritual life, which is eternal.

The gift of God is eternal life through Jesus Christ our Lord (Romans 6:23; see also Romans 8:10; Ephesians 2:4–5; John 10:27–28).

3. This God is the true god

He is called "true" to distinguish him from the idols and false gods of the heathen.

And this is eternal life, that they may know You, the

only true God, and Jesus Christ whom You have sent (John 17:3 NKJV).

The word "true" is used here in the sense of real or genuine. Any so-called god who is different from the God presented in the Bible is a counterfeit. (Read 2 Kings 19:17–18; Acts 14:11–15.)

Ought not such a God as this be respected, feared, trusted, glorified, loved, and obeyed?

3

What the Bible Says about the Trinity

In the last chapter we saw that there is only one God. In this chapter we learn that the one God exists in three Persons—the Father, the Son, and the Holy Spirit. This is called the doctrine of the Trinity. Although the word *Trinity* is not in the Bible, it expresses a scriptural truth; in fact, it was coined by one of the early Latin Christian writers to set forth the truth that God is a Tri-unity of Persons.

The term *Godhead* (Godhood) refers to God's essence or

divine Being; and it is a proper statement of truth to say that there are three Persons in the Godhead.

The Old Testament emphasizes the unity of God; that is, it asserts that there is but one God, in contrast to the many false gods of the heathen; nevertheless, there are intimations in the Old Testament of the fact that God exists in a plurality or Trinity of Persons. For example, the Spirit of God is mentioned in Genesis 1:2; the Son is mentioned in Psalm 2:7, 12; and there are plural expressions in a number of places that show that God is a Trinity.

> And God said, "Let us make man in our image, after our likeness" (Genesis 1:26).

The New Testament, while fully recognizing the unity of God, emphasizes the fact of the three Persons.

THREE PERSONS—ONE GOD

The Bible presents to us a Father who is God (John 3:16), a Son who is God (Philippians 2:5–8; John 1:1), and a Holy Spirit who is God (Acts 5:3–4); yet these are not three Gods, but one and the same God.

It is difficult, if not impossible, to explain what the word *Person* means as applied to the Father, the Son, and the Holy Spirit. We are accustomed to think of persons as individual human beings, and we know that three persons cannot be one being. The Persons of the Godhead are clearly distinguished from one another in many passages of Scripture; yet they cannot be separated. This truth is beyond complete understanding by our finite minds.

No illustration of the Trinity will suffice to explain this relationship, but we can perhaps get some help by trying to express the relationship mathematically. Men would ordinarily say of the Persons: one plus one plus one equals three. But it would be more accurate to say: one times one times one equals one, for each of the Persons is fully God in the absolute sense, and the three together are the one self-same God.

It is not possible for us to explain this truth fully, but it is necessary to know and to state clearly what the Bible actually says.

Throughout the Scriptures the Gospel message is plain: God the Father sent his Son to redeem fallen man; the Son willingly came to die for the sins of the world; and the Holy Spirit convicts of sin, regenerates the heart by the Word of God that he inspired, and takes the things of Christ and shows them to those who love him (see John 16:12–15).

Colossians 2:9 speaks very plainly:

In him [dwells] all the fullness of the Godhead bodily.

FURTHER BIBLE PROOF OF THE TRINITY

We have already alluded to some Bible proofs of the Trinity. One of these is the use of the plural in reference to God. In creating man, God said, "Let us make man in our image" (Genesis 1:26). If there were only one Person in the Godhead, does it not seem unlikely that God would use the words "us" and "our" in this instance? Would he not have been more likely to say, "I will make man in my image? (See also Genesis 3:22.) Again, in Isaiah 6:8 God refers to himself as "I" and "us," indicating both unity and plurality in the same Being.

Another Bible proof of the Trinity that has already been

mentioned is the fact that each of the Persons is individually called God.

Some further proofs may be listed this way:

1. Comparison of Scripture with Scripture

The passage in Isaiah 6 mentioned previously is still more interesting and presents a stronger proof of the Trinity when compared with John 12:35–41 and Acts 28:25–27.

In John 12:35–36, Christ is speaking about himself. Verse 37 tells us that the people to whom he spoke did not believe in him, even though he had performed many miracles before them. Then in verses 38–40 John quotes Isaiah 53:1 and 6:10 (written about 700 years before Christ was born), stating that Isaiah had foretold that some people would not believe in him, because they would harden their hearts against him. And John says plainly that the God whom Isaiah saw was the Lord Jesus: "Esaias . . . saw his glory" (v. 41).

In Acts 28:23 Paul was speaking to the people about Christ, but some of them did not believe in him. In verses 25–27 Isaiah 6:8–10 is again referred to—this time as the voice of the Holy Spirit (v. 25).

So we see how this one passage from Isaiah, when compared with these two New Testament references, brings out the truth that there are three Persons in one God.

2. The manifestation of the trinity at the baptism of Jesus

Let us turn now to Matthew 3:16–17. Here we have a beautiful picture painted for us, as well as a proof text given. Though we may forget every other Scripture evidence of the Trinity, it will not be easy to forget this once it is imprinted upon our minds. There is the blessed Jesus, the second Person of the Trinity, standing in the water, having been baptized by John. And now, behold, the heavens open, and the Spirit of God, the third Person of the Trinity, descends like a dove upon Jesus. But hearken! A voice is heard from heaven, the voice of the Father, the first Person of the Trinity, saying, "This is my beloved Son!" What clearer and better proof can we have than this that in the Godhead there are three Persons—the Father, the Son, and the Holy Spirit?

3. *Christ's declaration regarding the trinity in his Great Commission to his disciples*

"Go . . . teach all nations, baptizing them in the name of the Father, and of the Son, and of the Holy [Spirit]" (Matthew 28:19).

If these three were not God, it would not seem right to give each the same dignity and honor. And if they were more than one God, would not Jesus have been likely to say "in the names" instead of only "in the name"?

4. *Paul's statement in the apostolic benediction*

The grace of the Lord Jesus Christ, and the love of God, and the communion of the Holy [Spirit], be with you all. Amen (2 Corinthians 13:14).

If these three Persons here mentioned were not equally God it would not seem right to give each of them the same importance. Indeed, would it not be an insult to the true God to do this?

There are many other similar passages, but these are sufficient for our purpose here.

FAITH BELIEVES WHAT THE HUMAN INTELLECT CANNOT EXPLAIN

"Now faith is the substance of things hoped for, the evidence of things not seen" (Hebrews 11:1).

Perhaps after reading and thinking about these statements of the Scripture regarding the Trinity you are ready to exclaim, "This is a great mystery; I cannot understand it!" That is what everyone else says. And we are not required to understand it. He asks us only to believe it on the testimony of his own Word. There are a great many things in the Bible, and out of it, which we believe but do not understand. For example, we believe that God created the earth and everything in it, but we do not understand how he did it. Neither do we understand why a little brown seed planted in the black soil pushes a little green shoot up through the ground and brings forth a red flower—yet we believe it.

Then again, let us ask the question: Can you put the whole of the Atlantic Ocean in a teacup? No more can you expect to put the whole of the idea of God into a human brain.

Can you search out the deep things of God? Can you find out the limits of the Almighty? They are higher than heaven—what can you do? Deeper than Sheol— what can you know? Their measure is longer than the earth and broader than the sea (Job 11:7–9 NKJV).

O the depth of the riches both of the wisdom and knowledge of God! How unsearchable are his judgments, and his ways past finding out! (Romans 11:33).

32

4

What the Bible Says about God's Relation to the World

Men have always asked philosophical questions about the world. Here are four of the most important ones:

Where did the world come from?

What holds the world together and keeps it on its way?

Is there any order or government in the world?

Is there purpose in the world?

These four problems—of origin, of continuation, of direction, and of goal—cannot be answered by human philosophies. The Bible, however, gives the answer and shows that in every case that answer is *God*.

THE PROBLEM OF ORIGIN— GOD THE CREATOR

Where did the universe come from? The Bible tells us plainly in its opening sentence:

> In the beginning God created the heaven and the earth (Genesis 1:1).

The phrase "heaven and earth" means the universe, all that exists apart from God himself.

The answer, then, to the problem of origin is that there is an Almighty Creator, who called into existence that which had no previous existence.

> Through faith we understand that the worlds were framed by the word of God, so that things which are seen were not made of things which do appear (Hebrews 11:3).

This teaching of the Bible is in contrast and contradiction to the false theory of evolution, which is popular in the world today, but which really has no answer to the problem of beginning or origin. The materialistic evolutionist somehow imagines that matter always has existed in some form, for he will not admit a Creator. He traces the present forms back to earlier forms, but never actually explains how there came to be matter in the first place. He believes that by chance, in the same generation, both male and female of a species spontaneously appeared. He ridicules the Christian's faith in God and puts his faith in evolution.

But which is more reasonable: to believe that all things were created by an infinite, eternal, omnipotent Spirit—who is God—or to believe that matter always existed? There is no other alternative.

The Bible declares that God created everything by his powerful word.

> By the word of the LORD the heavens were made; And all the host of them by the breath of His mouth. . . . For He spoke, and it was done; He commanded, and it stood fast (Psalm 33:6, 9 NKJV).

It is interesting to remember that Christ is called the Word of God and that the New Testament speaks of him as the Creator.

> All things were made by him; and without him was not anything made that was made (John 1:3; see also Colossians 1:15–16; Hebrews 1:2).

As it came from the creative hand of God, the world was very good (Genesis 1:31). Sin came in afterward. All the evil we have ever seen or known or heard about in this world has come from sin.

THE PROBLEM OF PRESERVATION— GOD THE SUSTAINER

God not only made the world, but he holds it together

35

and keeps all things working in it. He does this in the same way in which he made it, that is, by his Word. This world has not been thrown into space and then left to take care of itself the best way it could.

> No mere machine is nature,
> Wound up and left to play,
> No wind harp swept at random
> By airs that idly stray:
> A Spirit sways the music;
> A hand is on the chords;
> Oh, bow thy head and listen!
> That hand—it is the Lord's!

It would be foolish to think that the universe created itself, and just as foolish to think that it can sustain itself. Isaiah 40:6–31 tells us about God as the Sustainer. The New Testament shows that, as in creation, Christ's hand is present in preservation.

> By him all things consist [hold together]" (Colossians 1:17). ". . . upholding all things by the word of his power (Hebrews 1:3).

THE PROBLEM OF DIRECTION— GOD THE GOVERNOR

Many unbelieving men maintain that there is only accident or chance in the world. Here, as in so many other instances, the devil has blinded the minds of men. Is it easier to believe that this complicated universe proceeds by blind chance, or that the almighty, all-wise God rules it and gives it direction? Scripture tells us clearly that God is the sovereign Ruler of the universe.

36

> The LORD has established His throne in heaven, and
> His kingdom rules over all (Psalm 103:19 NKJV).

We see in Genesis 3:1–19 the ruling hand of God in relationship to men, to Satan, and to the earth. Man's responsibility under the authority of God is plainly set forth. In Genesis 6 the history of the development of human wickedness and the consequent judgment of God in the Flood reveals the reigning hand of God. God's commands to Noah in Genesis 9 also show this sovereignty. Daniel recognized God's rulership of the world (Daniel 2:19–22; see also Ecclesiastes 11:9; 12:14; Romans 14:11–12).

Since God has made us, we belong to him, and he may do with us as he pleases.

To reconcile this with the Bible's teaching that man has a free will is beyond the capability of our finite minds. The Bible says:

> The secret things belong unto the LORD our God: but
> those things which are revealed belong unto us and
> to our children forever (Deuteronomy 29:29).

The relationship between God's sovereignty and man's freedom is one of God's secret things.

> But indeed, O man, who are you to reply against
> God? Will the thing formed say to him who formed
> it, "Why have you made me like this?" Does not the
> potter have power over the clay, from the same lump
> to make one vessel for honor and another for dis-
> honor? (Romans 9:20–21 NKJV).

This is not a cause for terror to the one who knows and trusts God; it is rather a cause for rejoicing, for we know that the sovereign Ruler of the universe is the One whose character is perfect in holiness and love. Because God made us and all the rest of the world, we need not fear the power of any creature.

> The angel of the LORD encamps all around those who fear Him, and delivers them (Psalm 34:7 NKJV).

> "No weapon formed against you shall prosper, And every tongue which rises against you in judgment You shall condemn. This is the heritage of the servants of the LORD, and their righteousness is from Me," says the LORD (Isaiah 54:17 NKJV).

From all this we may learn how perfectly secure the child of God is from all danger, and how well he is provided for in the world.

> "For the eyes of the LORD run to and fro throughout the whole earth, to show himself strong in the behalf of them whose heart is perfect toward him" (2 Chronicles 16:9).

> Look at the birds of the air, for they neither sow nor reap nor gather into barns; yet your heavenly Father feeds them. Are you not of more value than they? (Matthew 6:26 NKJV; compare Luke 12:6–7).

THE PROBLEM OF PURPOSE OR GOAL— GOD THE SAVIOR

Is there purpose in the universe? Is there a goal toward which the whole creation moves? In 2 Peter 3:1–15 we find that God is not only the Creator, Preserver, and Governor of the universe, but also its Savior. Because sin has besmirched the universe, God is working out his plan to deliver the universe from the bondage of corruption and to create "new heavens and a new earth, wherein [dwells] righteousness" (2 Peter 3:13). Then the universe will be delivered from the sorrow that now envelops it.

> Because the creation itself also will be delivered from the bondage of corruption into the glorious liberty of the children of God. For we know that the whole creation groans and labors with birth pangs together until now. (Romans 8:21–22 NKJV).

> And I saw a new heaven and a new earth (Revelation 21:1; see also Colossians 1:16–20).

This does not mean that all men will be saved. Personal salvation is only through the Lord Jesus Christ, and the deliverance of the material universe from the bondage of sin will come only through him.

This is a brief glance at the relationship between God and the world. It is in sharp contrast to human philosophies, which either would separate the universe from God altogether or would make God and the universe identical. The Bible gives the only satisfactory solution to these ever recurring problems—the problem of origin, the problem of preservation, the problem of direction, and the problem of purpose.

5

What the Bible Says about Creation and the Fall

To advertise its product, a certain paint company illustrates what its paint will do by showing "before and after" pictures. They demonstrate how their paint can transform a drab, unattractive room into one that is bright and cheerful. In this chapter, the picture is just the reverse. Here we will see the brightness of man when he came from the hand of God contrasted with the darkness that followed when he listened to Satan.

GOD CREATED MAN IN HIS OWN IMAGE
(Genesis 1:26–27)

We have seen that God is a moral, personal Being. When the Bible declares that man is made in the image of God, it evidently means that man is a moral personality. Personality involves self-consciousness and self-determination. You are conscious of yourself as an individual and as distinct from all other individuals, and you have the power to exercise your will; these facts are true because you are a person and, to that extent, made in the image of the personal God.

The account of the creation of man in Genesis 1 is a general statement of the fact of creation; the account in Genesis 2 is a more particular account of the method that God used.

> And the LORD God formed man of the dust of the ground, and breathed into his nostrils the breath of life; and man became a living soul (Genesis 2:7).

From this passage and from others it appears that man has a threefold nature. It is clear that the part of man formed from the ground was his body. We realize today that a number of the chemical elements that are found in the soil (such as carbon, hydrogen, oxygen, nitrogen, and others) are found also in the human body. The word that is translated "breath" is sometimes translated "spirit"; and the statement is made that "man became a living soul." The New Testament mentions these same three parts of man's being.

> I pray God your whole spirit and soul and body be

preserved blameless unto the coming of our Lord
Jesus Christ (I Thessalonians 5:23).

While it must be admitted that sometimes in Scripture
the terms *spirit* and *soul* are used interchangeably, there
are other passages, such as those just quoted, in which a
distinction is made between the two. When used without
distinction, both terms refer to that in man that is imma-
terial in contrast to his body, which is material. When,
however, a sharper analysis is made, the spirit is seen to
be that part of man which gives him God-consciousness,
which enables him to worship and love God and to have
fellowship with him. Animals do not have this capacity,
for they were not made in the image and likeness of God.

As a living soul, a self-conscious being, man has power
to think and reason and power to give expression to his
emotions. He has intellect, emotions, and will. Adam
exercised his power of thought when he gave names to all
the animals that God had created (Genesis 2:19).

God made man innocent; yet having a free will, man
had the choice of obeying or disobeying God (Genesis
2:16–17).

The very fact that man was made in the image of God
ruled out the possibility of man's being a mere machine
or robot. God did not create men as entirely separate
individuals, but he created man as a race—"male and
female created he them" (Genesis 1:27). Thus all human
beings who ever lived or who ever will live are related to
one another (Acts 17:26).

God created man with dominion over the whole earth
and all its creatures.

Then God blessed them, and God said to them, "Be
fruitful and multiply; fill the earth and subdue it; have

dominion over the fish of the sea, over the birds of the air, and over every living thing that moves on the earth" (Genesis 1:28 NKJV).

Psalm 8 speaks of this dominion that man had from God and that has been largely lost through sin. In Hebrews 2:5–10, the inspired writer quotes from this psalm to show how it also predicted the coming Savior, and to teach us that, when he rules in righteousness and peace over the earth, he will exercise all the power over his creation that Adam lost through sin and more! By the grace of God redeemed sinners will share in that glorious reign of the King of righteousness and of peace.

GOD'S PURPOSE IN CREATING MAN

What object did God have in view in putting man on the earth? Was it only that man might have a good time in his own way and do as he pleased in all things? Was man made for his own sake, or was he made for the sake of someone else? Surely the very fact that God made man in his own image and likeness proves that he wanted man to have fellowship with him and worship him. He wanted man to love, serve, and obey him.

> For none of us lives to himself, and no one dies to himself. For if we live, we live to the Lord; and if we die, we die to the Lord. Therefore, whether we live or die, we are the Lord's (Romans 14:7-8 NKJV).

> You are worthy, O Lord, to receive glory and honor and power; for You created all things, and by Your will they exist and were created (Revelation 4:11 NKJV).

> That he no longer should live the rest of his time in

the flesh to the lusts of men, but to the will of God (1 Peter 4:2; see also 2 Corinthians 5:15; 1 Corinthians 6:19–20; Galatians 2:20).

Then, again, while God wants us to please him in all things, he tells us that, if we seek to do his will, we shall find our chief joy in doing that very thing. God knew that we should need enjoyment, and he lovingly gave us the best there was in the universe to enjoy—he gave us himself!

After these things the word of the LORD came to Abram in a vision, saying, "Do not be afraid, Abram. I am your shield, your exceedingly great reward" (Genesis 15:1 NKJV).

"The LORD is my portion," says my soul, "Therefore I hope in Him!" (Lamentations 3:24 NKJV).

So He said to them, "Assuredly, I say to you, there is no one who has left house or parents or brothers or wife or children, for the sake of the kingdom of God, who shall not receive many times more in this present time, and in the age to come eternal life" (Luke 18:29–30 NKJV; see also Philippians 3:7–8; Psalm 16:5).

MAN'S MORAL TEST IN EDEN

Then the LORD God took the man and put him in the garden of Eden to tend and keep it. And the LORD God commanded the man, saying, "Of every tree of the garden you may freely eat; but of the tree of the knowledge of good and evil you shall not eat, for in the day that you eat of it you shall surely die" (Genesis 2 :15–17 NKJV).

This was a very simple command, but it was enough to test man's obedience to God. Here in an uncomplicated way, with man in a lovely environment and with all his needs supplied, the question was to be decided whether man would obey God or not. Would he stay within the bounds God had set or go beyond? That the issue was so simple makes the disobedience all the more tragic.

THE FALL OF MAN

Our first parents disobeyed God's command. God gave them liberty to choose between good and evil. They chose evil and so fell from their state of innocence by sinning against God. The way in which they came to do this is stated at length in Genesis 3, especially verse 6:

> And when the woman saw that the tree was good for food, and that it was pleasant to the eyes, and a tree to be desired to make one wise, she took of the fruit thereof, and did eat, and gave also unto her husband with her; and he did eat.

It is interesting to note that, in the New Testament, Paul deals with this account as the description of an actual, historical event (Romans 5:12).

A parallel passage is 1 John 2:16, where the world is said to consist of the "lust of the flesh, and the lust of the eyes, and the pride of life," the same three elements that were present in the temptation of Eve. Now this teaches us that the best of us ought not to trust in our own strength to resist Satan, but, rather, to trust in God! Adam was created innocent, and yet he was not strong enough to resist this temptation. How much weaker therefore must we be in our state of sin!

Not that we are sufficient of ourselves to think any thing as of ourselves; but our sufficiency is of God (2 Corinthians 3:5).

The great mistake that our first parents made was that they did not believe God; they failed to trust in his word.

But without faith it is impossible to please Him, for he who comes to God must believe that He is, and that He is a rewarder of those who diligently seek Him (Hebrews 11:6 NKJV).

THE RESULTS OF THE FALL

God told Adam and Eve that if they ate of the forbidden fruit, in that day they would surely die. Yet afterward they lived nearly a thousand years! (See Genesis 5:1–5.) How are we to explain this? By noting that there are two kinds of death. There is not only a natural death, a death of the body; but there is also a spiritual death.

And you He made alive, who were dead in trespasses and sins (Ephesians 2:1 NKJV).

Their spiritual death took place that very day, as indicated by Genesis 3:8, which says that they tried to hide themselves from the presence of God. It is reasonable to believe that decay began in their bodies at this time, of which they later died.

The Bible tells us about hell, a place where the wicked will go and be punished eternally. Scripture calls this the "second death" (Revelation 20:14–15). But God does not want men to go there. He did not make them for that. He made them to enjoy him, not only in this world, but also in that which is to come.

"For I have no pleasure in the death of one who dies," says the Lord GOD. "Therefore turn and live!" (Ezekiel 18:32 NKJV; read 2 Peter 3:9).

Just think of it, an eternity of enjoyment is before those who have begun to enjoy God here! Have you yet begun to enjoy him?

6

What the Bible Says about Sin

It has been said that those who have a light view of sin will have little appreciation of salvation. If we are ever tempted to minimize the awfulness of sin, we should remember that it was sin that made it necessary for the Lord Jesus Christ, the Son of God, to become a man and die upon the cross.

Some people try to get rid of sin by denying its existence altogether. However, the Bible declares that it is a terrible reality.

WHAT IS SIN?

1. Sin is the transgression of the law of God

The Bible tells us that sin is the breaking of God's law. Whoever breaks the law of God, whoever does anything God told him not to do, or whoever fails to do anything God told him to do, has committed sin.

> Everyone who practices sin also practices lawlessness; and sin is lawlessness" (I John 3:4 NASB).

> Therefore, to him who knows to do good and does not do it, to him it is sin (James 4:17 NKJV).

It is well for us to understand what is meant by the law of God. Perhaps we think that only the Ten Commandments are meant; but if we look at Romans 2:13–15, especially verse 15, we will see that God has written a law in the hearts of men. We all know what that law is. We all know when we break that law. Every time we do wrong there is something within us called conscience that tells us so. Perhaps if we could count up the number of times conscience has accused us, we might be able to know what great sinners we are.

2. Sin is a falling away from God

Sin is something more than merely transgressing or breaking God's law. It is also a falling away from God. Look at Adam and Eve; having sinned, they tried at once to hide themselves from their Creator. They feared God at that moment. They did not want to see him and commune with him as they had done before. And this is true of all sinners before they find Christ.

50

And this is the condemnation, that the light has come
into the world, and men loved darkness rather than
light, because their deeds were evil. For everyone
practicing evil hates the light and does not come to
the light, lest his deeds should be exposed (John
3:19–20 NKJV).

The sinner would destroy God if he could. He may not
be willing to admit this; he may not really be aware of it;
but it is a fact that, if sin had its own way forever, it would
drag the Almighty from his throne in the heavens.

But the carnal mind is enmity against God: for it is
not subject to the law of God, neither indeed can be
(Romans 8:7).

THE UNIVERSALITY OF SIN

Having learned what sin is, we are now brought face to
face with the awful fact that by their fall, that is, by
breaking God's commandment, our first parents brought
all mankind into a state of sin and misery. They could not
keep their son Cain from murder, for he was born a sinner.
And thus sin has been passed on from generation to
generation.

They did not sin alone, but in them all the human race
sinned. They were like a fountain which, when it becomes
muddy, causes all the streams flowing from it to be muddy
too.

Wherefore, as by one man sin entered into the world,
and death by sin; and so death passed upon all men,
for that all have sinned" (Romans 5:12; compare
Genesis 3:16–19, 22, 24 with Romans 5:12, 18–19).

SIN AND SINS

1. The sin nature

Because all of us were in Adam when he sinned, every human being who has been born into the world—except Jesus Christ—has been born with a sinful nature.

> By one man's disobedience many were made sinners (Romans 5:19).

This is sometimes spoken of as *original sin* or as *total depravity*.

Adam, the first head of all mankind, sinned and brought the whole race into pain, sorrow, death, and judgment. He was our representative. He stood in our place before God just as, later on, Jesus Christ, who is called in Scripture the "second man" (I Corinthians 15:47) and the "last Adam" (1 Corinthians 15:45), stood in our place before God. The Lord Jesus regained for us what Adam lost, even as the latter part of Romans 5:19 definitely states.

> By obedience of one shall many be made righteous.

We were born, as has been stated previously, with a sinful nature inherited from Adam.

> We . . . were by nature the children of wrath, even as others (Ephesians 2:3).

It may be some time after our birth before we begin to show that we are sinners, but we are so certain to show it as to leave no doubt that we were born sinful. We have all seen that a child does not need to be taught to sin. The reason is that he has inherited a sin nature from Adam, and so it is his nature to sin.

The term *total depravity* does not mean that every individual is as bad as he could be, but rather that the corruption of sin runs through our whole being, so that the Bible declares that those apart from Christ are "dead in trespasses and sins" (Ephesians 2:1). The sin of Adam is in our souls and spirits, as well as in our bodies.

> And GOD saw that the wickedness of man was great in the earth, and that every imagination of the thoughts of his heart was only evil continually (Genesis 6:5).

This total depravity may also be described as a lack of original righteousness. There is nothing within any of us by nature that could stand the test before the holy and righteous God.

> As it is written, There is none righteous, no, not one (Romans 3:10).

2. The fruit of the sin nature

From the original sin, which is our nature, come the sins that are manifest in our lives. We have not become sinners because we sinned, but we sin because we are sinners. Sins in our lives may be actual transgressions, or they may be the disobedience of not doing what God commands.

> For out of the heart proceed evil thoughts, murders, adulteries, fornications, thefts, false witness, blasphemies (Matthew 15:19. See also the description of men as sinners in Romans 3:9–20).

The fiendish evil displayed by civilized men in the wars of this century shows the folly of the idea that man is gradually improving morally.

All of this proves the necessity of what the Lord Jesus said to Nicodemus:

> Jesus answered and said to him, "Most assuredly, I say to you, unless one is born again, he cannot see the kingdom of God" (John 3:3 NKJV).

FIVE RESULTS OF SIN

1. Loss of communion with God

> And you, that were sometime alienated and enemies in your mind by wicked works, yet now [has] he reconciled (Colossians 1:21).

Loss of communion with God means our separation from him through sin and disobedience. This is described in Scripture as spiritual death (Ephesians 2:1). As soon as Adam and Eve sinned, their fellowship with God was broken; they could not stand in his holy presence unashamed and unafraid. Neither could the holy God tolerate sin!

> So he drove out the man; and he placed at the east of the garden of Eden cherubims, and a flaming sword which turned every way, to keep the way of the tree of life (Genesis 3:24).

God could not talk with them as he had done before. They were now separated from him; and all men have been thus separated from God in spirit ever since. Nor can they be brought back into fellowship or communion with him except through the one Mediator, Jesus Christ.

2. The condemnation of God

Condemnation implies blame. God holds us accountable for our sin. We are like criminals who have been tried, found guilty, and sentenced to be punished. In this sense every one of us is already lost, unless born again by faith in the Lord Jesus Christ.

> He who believes in Him is not condemned; but he who does not believe is condemned already, because he has not believed in the name of the only begotten Son of God (John 3:18 NKJV).

> He who believes in the Son has everlasting life; and he who does not believe the Son shall not see life, but the wrath of God abides on him (John 3:36 NKJV).

3. Earthly unhappiness

All the unhappiness in this world is part of the misery of sin. We would never have known sorrow, sadness, and death, but for the Fall. This does not mean that individual sinners are always unhappy. The psalmist was troubled when he saw the wicked prospering, as is often the case temporarily. He was reminded, however, by the Spirit of God, of "their end." (See Psalm 73, especially verse 17.)

4. Death

Death, whether spiritual or physical, is the result of sin. Paul shows in Romans 5:12–21 how Adam's sin caused death to reign; therefore, even infants, who have not committed personal sins, die. Physical death is the separation of the soul and spirit from the body. It is an "enemy" that will be destroyed when the Lord Jesus completes the resurrections, as described in 1 Corinthians 15.

> For the wages of sin is death; but the gift of God is eternal life through Jesus Christ our Lord (Romans 6:23).

5. Eternal punishment

This is a solemn fact of Scripture that cannot be ignored. If God is eternal and if the condition of the saved is eternal, then the punishment of the lost must be eternal, for the same word is used in reference to them all. The Lord Jesus Christ said more about hell than did anyone else in the Scripture. He wanted men to see their awful danger and to flee to him for refuge; but those who will not have him as their Savior must have him as their judge.

> Then He will also say to those on the left hand, "Depart from Me, you cursed, into the everlasting fire prepared for the devil and his angels" (Matthew 25:41 NKJV).

GOD'S REMEDY FOR SIN

This teaching about sin forms a black background against which the jewel of God's grace shines even more brightly. As the prophet Jonah declared, "Salvation is of the LORD" (Jonah 2:9). God manifested his love and grace by giving his Son, the Lord Jesus Christ, to be our Savior. Christ is the only One who can deliver men out of sin and misery and bring them into a state of salvation.

> But when the kindness and the love of God our Savior toward man appeared, not by works of righteousness which we have done, but according to His mercy He

saved us, through the washing of regeneration and renewing of the Holy Spirit, whom He poured out on us abundantly through Jesus Christ our Savior (Titus 3:4–6 NKJV).

The ground of our salvation is the redemptive work of Christ. The source of it is God's grace. The channel through which it is received is faith. God did not save men because they deserved it, or because they could demand his mercy, but simply because it was his good pleasure to do it.

For by grace you have been saved through faith, and that not of yourselves; it is the gift of God, not of works, lest anyone should boast (Ephesians 2:8–9 NKJV).

It has been said that grace is unmerited favor. But it is more than this, for the saved sinner receives the very opposite of what he deserves.

For God so loved the world that He gave His only begotten Son, that whoever believes in Him should not perish but have everlasting life (John 3:16 NKJV).

7

What the Bible Says about the Person of Christ

After the enemies of the Lord Jesus Christ had asked him questions in which they sought to trap him, he asked them a searching question: "What do you think about the Christ? Whose Son is He?" (Matthew 22:42 NKJV). This is the most important question ever to be faced by any individual, for the answer to this determines a person's eternal destiny. The teaching concerning the Person and work of Jesus Christ is the central teaching of the Word of

God. Here is the place to detect false or unsound doctrine in any cult or heresy.

> Beloved, do not believe every spirit, but test the spirits, whether they are of God; because many false prophets have gone out into the world. By this you know the Spirit of God: Every spirit that confesses that Jesus Christ has come in the flesh is of God, and every spirit that does not confess that Jesus Christ has come in the flesh is not of God. And this is the spirit of the Antichrist, which you have heard was coming, and is now already in the world (1 John 4:1–3 NKJV).

We need to be absolutely clear about what the Bible says concerning the Person of the Lord Jesus Christ.

JESUS CHRIST IS GOD

The Bible teaches that Jesus Christ is God in the full and absolute sense of the word, that he is one of the Persons of the holy Trinity. This teaching is called *the deity of Jesus Christ.* There are many proofs of the deity of Christ in Scripture. Following are five of the most prominent:

1. He is called God

Besides the divine names that are given to him—such as Immanuel ("God with us," Isaiah 7:14; Matthew 1:23). Scripture definitely states that Jesus Christ is God.

> In the beginning was the Word, and the Word was with God, and the Word was God (John 1:1).

This verse shows that the Son of God is as eternal as the Father, has his own personality, and is God as the Father is God.

But to the Son He says: "Your throne, O God, is forever and ever; a scepter of righteousness is the scepter of Your Kingdom" (Hebrews 1:8 NKJV).

We are in him that is true, even in his Son Jesus Christ. This is the true God, and eternal life (1 John 5:20; see also Romans 9:5; Colossians 1:15; Hebrews 1:2–3).

2. He has the attributes of God

The Bible describes Christ as eternal and unchangeable:

In the beginning was the Word (John 1:1)

Jesus Christ the same yesterday, today, and forever (Hebrews 13:8).

Like a cloak You will fold them up, and they will be changed. But You are the same, and Your years will not fail (Hebrews 1:12 NKJV).

Furthermore, the attributes of God that cannot belong to any creature are said to belong to Christ. He is omnipotent (all powerful) (Matthew 28:18; Hebrews 1:3). He is omniscient (all knowing) (John 1:48; 2:24–25; 21:17). He is omnipresent (present in all places at all times) (Matthew 28:20).

3. He was active in creation

We have seen in a previous chapter that God is the Creator. In a number of passages of Scripture Jesus Christ, the Son of God, is said to be the Creator.

All things were made by him; and without him was not anything made that was made (John 1:3; see also Colossians 1:16 and Hebrews 1:2).

4. He forgives sins

In Mark 2 when the Lord Jesus told the paralyzed man that his sins were forgiven, the scribes complained, saying:

Who can forgive sins but God only? (Mark 2:7).

They were correct in this respect, but wrong in not believing that Jesus is God, for he proved his right to forgive sins.

But that you may know that the Son of Man has power on earth to forgive sins—He said to the paralytic, "I say to you, arise, take up your bed, and go to your house." Immediately he arose, took up the bed, and went out in the presence of them all, so that all were amazed and glorified God, saying, "We never saw anything like this!" (Mark 2:10–12 NKJV).

S. He claimed to be God

To believe that Jesus is good, we must believe that he is God because he claimed to be. If he were lying, we cannot consider him good. His enemies understood that he was claiming deity and accused him of blasphemy. He said: "I and my Father are one" (John 10:30).

He who has seen Me has seen the Father (John 14:9 NKJV).

JESUS CHRIST BECAME MAN

An old fable tells about a man who tried to persuade some birds to come into his home out of the intense cold. Although the birds were freezing to death, they refused to come inside because they were afraid of the man. The man eventually realized that to save the birds he must become a bird and communicate with them in their own language. Since he was unable to do this, the birds died.

> The Word was made flesh, and dwelt among us (John 1:14).   -

Thus we see that the Lord Jesus Christ is one Person with two natures. He is the God-Man, possessing absolute deity and true humanity. His becoming man is often referred to as the *incarnation*.

1. His birth

The Son of God humbled himself by being born.

> Who, being in the form of God, thought it not robbery to be equal with God: but made himself of no reputation, and took upon him the form of a servant, and was made in the likeness of men (Philippians 2:6–7).

He always was the Lord of glory; by him the worlds were made; and yet he consented to take on human nature (Hebrews 2:14).

His mother was not a queen, but a poor maid of Nazareth. His birthplace was not a palace, but a stable. He doubtless had to work for a living. He lived poor and died poor.

> For you know the grace of our Lord Jesus Christ, that though He was rich, yet for your sakes He became poor, that you through His poverty might become rich (2 Corinthians 8:9 NKJV; see also Luke 2:7; Matthew 8:20; Mark 6:3).

This birth was a virgin birth, as Luke 1:34–35 shows:

63

Then said Mary unto the angel, How shall this be, seeing I know not a man? And the angel answered and said unto her, The Holy [Spirit] shall come upon [you], and the power of the Highest shall overshadow [you]; therefore also that holy thing which shall be born of [you] shall be called the Son of God.

2. His life

Even though he was the Son of God, Jesus escaped none of the trials of this life, apart from sin. He experienced the misery of poverty, as we have seen. He also knew the misery of being misunderstood by relatives and friends— "For even His brothers did not believe in Him" (John 7:5 NKJV).

We have not an high priest which cannot be touched with the feeling of our infirmities; but was in all points tempted like as we are, yet without sin [or, "apart from sin"] (Hebrews 4:15).

The ministry of Jesus was marked by teachings and miracles. All attempts to explain his miracles without acknowledging that Jesus possessed supernatural powers are unconvincing. The miracles are woven into the accounts of his life so closely that to deny them is to make the rest of the story meaningless.

It has been said that while some people might find the Bible easier to believe without the miracles of Jesus, it really would not be worth believing without them. The miracles show us that Jesus Christ truly came from God and is the Son of God.

3. His death

Although he was perfectly holy, the Lord Jesus was

reckoned by God as though he were a sinner. The Scripture teaches that our sin was imputed to him; that is, it was put to his account as though it were his own; it was laid upon and counted against him.

> He made Him who knew no sin to be sin on our behalf, that we might become the righteousness of God in Him (2 Corinthians 5:21 NASB).

> Who Himself bore our sins in His own body on the tree, that we, having died to sins, might live for righteousness—by whose stripes you were healed (1 Peter 2:24 NKJV; see also Isaiah 53:3–6).

What a terrible humiliation this was for a sinless soul to endure! The fact that he was the Sin-bearer caused him to be forsaken by the Father.

> And about the ninth hour Jesus cried out with a loud voice, saying, "Eli, Eli, lama sabachthani?" that is, "My God, My God, why have You forsaken Me?" (Matthew 27:46 NKJV)

Just what our Lord's forsaken cry on the cross means, no human can possibly know. We only know that it was part of the penalty of sin that he endured for us. It must have been the hardest part, harder than any of the insults or buffetings he received from men, harder even than the pains of crucifixion itself. But we may praise God for the fact that he abandoned his own Son for a time so that he would not have to abandon us forever.

Deity could not die; but because Jesus Christ is Man as well as God, he could die; and because he is God as well as Man, his death was the death of an infinite Person, and thus sufficient to satisfy the debt for every sin of every person who ever lived.

In contrast to some modern theories, the gospel writers clearly state that Jesus really died. Not only was a spear thrust into his side, but it was the Roman soldiers, well-acquainted with death by crucifixion, who bore witness to Jesus' death (John 19:33–34).

4. His resurrection

The Bible shows us that the humiliation of the Lord Jesus Christ led to his exaltation by God the Father. He accomplished what he came into the world to do and rose from the dead as our victorious Lord and Savior.

The empty tomb and Jesus' later appearances are two evidences of the resurrection. John, coming to the tomb, realized that Christ's body had not been stolen because the burial clothes were lying there as they had been wound around the body of Jesus. No one stealing a body would have left the graveclothes. As to his appearances, on one occasion more than five hundred persons saw him. It is highly unlikely that so many people would have been mistaken about whom they saw (John 20:6–8; 1 Corinthians 15:6).

8

What the Bible Says about the Work of Christ

Quicksand in a swamp in the southern part of our nation has claimed many lives. Some years ago, a highway was built that now carries thousands of travelers safely through that place of death. How foolish someone would be to use the old route when the new one is available.

One goal of the work of Christ is to bring men safely through death to spend eternity in heaven. The benefits of his work are available to all who will receive him in faith. In the work of redemption the Lord Jesus Christ fulfills the three-fold office of Prophet, Priest, and King.

CHRIST AS PROPHET

A prophet is a spokesman for God, one who speaks forth, one who declares a given message. In so doing he frequently tells of things to come.

Peter, guided by the Holy Spirit, said that Christ was the One of whom Moses wrote, saying:

> For Moses truly said to the fathers, "The LORD your God will raise up for you a Prophet like me from your brethren. Him you shall hear in all things, whatever He says to you." (Acts 3:22 NKJV; see also Deuteronomy 18:15–19; Hebrews 1:1–2; John 1:17–18).

As a prophet, Christ tells us how we may be saved from the guilt and punishment of sin. This he does through his Word as it is applied to our hearts by his Spirit.

1. His Word

> But these are written that you may believe that Jesus is the Christ, the Son of God, and that believing you may have life in His name (John 20:31 NKJV).

If we read God's Word, we will know how to be saved; for that, and that only, tells us.

2. His Holy Spirit

> But the Helper, the Holy Spirit, whom the Father will send in My name, He will teach you all things, and bring to your remembrance all things that I said to you (John 14:26 NKJV).

It is not of much use simply to read the Word of God unless we have the Holy Spirit to help us understand it, believe it, and obey it. We should always study the Bible with prayer for the Holy Spirit's enlightenment, he indwells every believer (John 14:16–17); and he is the Christian's infallible teacher (John 14:26; 15:26).

The best Scripture reference to substantiate that Christ continues even now to be a prophet is found in Revelation, chapters 1–3. Here he is represented, after his ascension into glory, as speaking to the seven churches in Asia, giving them instruction and telling them what will happen.

CHRIST AS PRIEST

A priest is one who represents men before God, who offers sacrifice for the sinner, and intercedes for him, a go-between or mediator between God and man. The Lord Jesus Christ is presented in the Bible, especially in the Epistle to the Hebrews, as our "great high priest" (Hebrews 4:14). He is our only priest, the only one who could offer a perfect sacrifice for our sins, and he "always lives to make intercession" for us (Hebrews 7:25 NKJV).

1. Christ as our priest offered a sacrifice

The animal sacrifices of the Old Testament, while ordained by God to be used temporarily as an atonement or covering for sin, could not take away the guilt and penalty of sin. They all pointed forward to the Lord Jesus Christ, who offered himself as our sacrifice.

John the Baptist, seeing Jesus, said:

> Behold! The Lamb of God who takes away the sin of the world! (John 1:29 NKJV).

69

Jesus' death as the Lamb of God was a substitutionary sacrifice. This is shown by his own declaration:

> The Son of man came not to be ministered unto, but to minister, and to give his life a ransom for many (Matthew 20:28).

The word *for* in the last phrase means "in place of." During the war in Vietnam an enemy hand grenade was thrown into the middle of a small group of American soldiers. One soldier threw himself on the grenade and was instantly killed as it exploded. He chose to die that his friends might live. This is but a faint illustration of the substitutionary death of the Lord Jesus Christ.

Christ was both the offerer and the offering, both the priest and the sacrifice. In giving himself to die on the cross, he accomplished the work for which he came into the world. This atoning work is often referred to as the *finished work* of Christ. It includes three major elements.

a. *Propitiation.* By his death the Lord Jesus Christ satisfied divine justice and made up for the dishonor that the sin of man had put upon God's name and authority. This is the meaning of propitiation. The holy God could not save sinners apart from a righteous ground, for he cannot compromise with sin. That righteous ground—the death of God's Son—had been in the plan of God from all eternity (1 Peter 1:20).

> Whom God set forth as a propitiation by His blood, through faith, to demonstrate His righteousness, because in His forbearance God had passed over the sins that were previously committed, to demonstrate at the present time His righteousness, that He might be

just and the justifier of the one who has faith in Jesus (Romans 3:25–26 NKJV).

And he is the propitiation for our sins: and not for ours only, but also for the sins of the whole world (1 John 2:2 NKJV).

b. *Redemption.* The Bible teaches that sin has placed men under a terrible bondage from which the Lord Jesus, by his death, redeems them.

For all have sinned, and come short of the glory of God; being justified freely by his grace through the redemption that is in Christ Jesus (Romans 3:23–24; see also Ephesians 1:7; Colossians 1:14).

The price of our redemption was the blood of Christ.

Knowing that you were not redeemed with corruptible things, like silver or gold, from your aimless conduct received by tradition from your fathers, but with the precious blood of Christ, as of a lamb without blemish and without spot (1 Peter 1:18–19 NKJV)

The church of God, which he [has] purchased with his own blood (Acts 20:28; see also 1 Corinthians 6:19–20).

c. *Reconciliation.* By his death the Lord Jesus Christ reconciled men to God; that is, those who were enemies were made friends. This reconciliation has been made for all men but does not become actual in the life of an individual until he accepts Christ.

When we were enemies, we were reconciled to God by the death of his Son (Romans 5:10).

> Now all things are of God, who has reconciled us to Himself through Jesus Christ, and has given us the ministry of reconciliation, that is, that God was in Christ reconciling the world to Himself, not imputing their trespasses to them, and has committed to us the word of reconciliation. Now then, we are ambassadors for Christ, as though God were pleading through us: we implore you on Christ's behalf, be reconciled to God (2 Corinthians 5:18–20).

2. Christ as our priest makes intercession for us

Christ's work of atonement has been completed once and for all. On the cross he said, "It is finished" (John 19:30). There is no good work any man needs to add to Christ's work of salvation.

He continues now as our Great High Priest. His intercessory prayer, recorded in John 17, tells us something of his ministry for us at the throne of grace.

> But He, because He continues forever, has an unchangeable priesthood. Therefore He is also able to save to the uttermost those who come to God through Him, since He always lives to make intercession for them (Hebrews 7:24–25 NKJV).

> Who *is* he that condemns? *It is* Christ who died, and furthermore is also risen, who is even at the right hand of God, who also makes intercession for us (Romans 8:34 NKJV).

CHRIST AS KING

There is much said in the Scripture about the kingship of Jesus Christ.

1. When he was on earth the first time, he was announced as a King

"Now when Jesus was born in Bethlehem of Judea in the days of Herod the king, behold, there came wise men from the east to Jerusalem, saying, Where is he that is born King of the Jews?" (Matthew 2:1–2; see also John 1:49).

When John the Baptist began preaching, he proclaimed that the kingdom of God was at hand. The Lord Jesus proclaimed the same message. In his public entry into Jerusalem near the end of his earthly ministry, Christ formally offered himself as the King, in fulfillment of Old Testament prophecy.

All this was done that it might be fulfilled which was spoken by the prophet, saying: "Tell the daughter of Zion, 'Behold, your King is coming to you, Lowly, and sitting on a donkey, A colt, the foal of a donkey'" (Matthew 21:4–5 NKJV).

He was rejected by the nation of Israel and was crucified as the "King of the Jews" (Matthew 27:37; Mark 15:26; Luke 23:38; John 19:19–22).

Anticipating his rejection, the Lord Jesus declared his purpose to build his Church—to be composed of both Jews and Gentiles.

There is neither Greek nor Jew, circumcision nor uncircumcision, Barbarian, Scythian, bond nor free: but Christ is all, and in all (Colossians 3:11).

There is neither Jew nor Greek, there is neither slave nor free, there is neither male nor female: for you are all one in Christ Jesus (Galatians 3:28 NKJV).

He came unto his own, and his own received him not. But as many as received him, to them gave he power to become the sons of God, even to them that believe on his name" (John 1:11–12).

And I also say to you that you are Peter, and on this rock I will build My church, and the gates of Hades shall not prevail against it (Matthew 16:18 NKJV).

2. Christ is the Head of the church

While Christ is not called in the Bible the "King of the church," he is called its "Head." It is evident that he is sovereign over everyone who belongs to him. He is the Lord who is to be obeyed.

And [has] put all things under his feet, and gave him to be head over all things to the church, which is his body, the fullness of him that [fills] all in all" (Ephesians 1:22–23).

It is the enemies of Christ who refuse him the sovereignty that is rightfully his. He taught this in a parable.

But his citizens hated him, and sent a message after him, saying, We will not have this man to reign over us (Luke 19:14; see also v. 27).

3. Christ is coming to the earth again to set up his kingdom.

This is God's purpose as expressed in many prophecies, both in the Old and New Testaments.

And the LORD shall be king over all the earth: in that day shall there be one LORD, and his name one (Zechariah 14:9).

74

Describing the glorious return of Christ to earth the book of Revelation says:

> Now out of His mouth goes a sharp sword, that with it He should strike the nations. And He Himself will rule them with a rod of iron. He Himself treads the winepress of the fierceness and wrath of Almighty God. And He has on His robe and on His thigh a name written: KING OF KINGS AND LORD OF LORDS (Revelation 19:15–16 NKJV; see also 11:15; Daniel 7:13–14).

In the time of his kingdom there will be righteousness and peace and prosperity over all the earth.

> The wolf and the lamb shall feed together, and the lion shall eat straw like the bullock: and dust shall be the serpent's meat. They shall not hurt nor destroy in all my holy mountain (Isaiah 65:25 NKJV; see also 11:6–9; Ezekiel 34:24–26).

During the millennial kingdom Christ will be acknowledged by all as King of kings and Lord of lords.

In Christ as Prophet we have the will of God revealed to us. In Christ as Priest we have pardon and acceptance with God. In Christ as King we have deliverance from all enemies, even Satan himself. In Christ, therefore, we are complete.

> And you are complete in Him, who is the head of all principality and power (Colossians 2:10 NKJV).

9

What the Bible Says about the Holy Spirit

THE HOLY SPIRIT IS A PERSON IN THE GODHEAD

The Holy Spirit is one of the three Persons of the Godhead, not a mere influence as some false teachers claim. From the many infallible proofs of his personality, the following are particularly striking:

1. His names imply personality as well as deity

He is linked with the Father and the Son in such passages as the baptismal formula (Matthew 28:19) and the apostolic benediction (2 Corinthians 13:14). He is called "the Lord, the Spirit" (2 Corinthians 3:18, NASB); "the eternal Spirit" (Hebrews 9:14); "the Spirit of God" (Genesis 1:2); "the Spirit of Christ" (Romans 8:9); "the Comforter" (John 16:7). These are typical of the titles by which the Scriptures teach that the Holy Spirit is a person, one with the Father and the Son. (The word *Spirit* is more appropriate in modern English than *Ghost*, which occurs often in the King James Version of the Bible and which is still retained in many of our hymns.)

2. *Personal pronouns are used in reference to him*

No one would think of referring to God the Father or to God the Son as "it"; yet many people say "it" in reference to the Holy Spirit. This is partly caused by several misleading translations in the King James Version (compare Romans 8:16, 26 in the KJV and the NASB). The personality of the Holy Spirit is clearly shown by the use of the masculine personal pronoun in the words of the Lord Jesus concerning the Holy Spirit in John 14–16; this is correctly translated in the English versions by the personal pronoun "he" (John 14:16–17, 26; 15:26; 16:8, 13).

3. *His words and deeds prove his personality*

Only persons think, speak, and act. The words and deeds ascribed to the Holy Spirit in the Bible could not have been spoken or performed by an impersonal force or influence. Note some of his words and deeds:

a. He spoke to men of old (Acts 1:16; Hebrews 3:7).

b. He performed miracles (Acts 2:4; 8:39).

c. He appointed "overseers to feed the church of God" (Acts 20:28).

d. He guided the apostles and their fellow workers in their ministry (Acts 11: 12; 13:2; 16:6–7).

e. "The Spirit Himself bears witness with our spirit that we are children of God" (Romans 8:16 NASB).

f. "The Spirit Himself intercedes for us" (Romans 8:26 NASB).

4. Man's attitude toward him evidences his personality

a. The Lord Jesus said that the unsaved could blaspheme the Holy Spirit (Mark 3:29). *They can also resist him* (Acts 7:51).

b. Christians can grieve him (Ephesians 4:30), *quench him* (1 Thessalonians 5:19), *or be filled with the Spirit* (Ephesians 5:18).

THE HOLY SPIRIT WROTE THE BIBLE THROUGH GODLY MEN OF OLD

The Holy Spirit is the particular person of the Godhead who produced the Scriptures (2 Timothy 3:16).

> "For no prophecy was ever made by an act of human will, but men moved by the Holy Spirit spoke from God" (2 Peter 1:21 NASB; see also 2 Samuel 23:2).

THE HOLY SPIRIT CONVICTS THE WORLD OF SIN, OF RIGHTEOUSNESS, AND OF JUDGMENT (John 16:8–11)

One might think that our sinfulness would be so evident that we would not need the Holy Spirit to convince us that we are sinners; but we do need him to convict us that we lack righteousness (which God requires and which is found only in Jesus Christ) and deserve judgment. This is a point on which many are deceived. Too many of us think more highly of ourselves than we ought to think; and as long as we make this mistake, we will not realize our need of a Savior. Yet until we acknowledge our need of him, we will not look to him for salvation! How thankful we ought to be, therefore, that the Holy Spirit convinces us of sin. Otherwise, we would be like people dying of a disease of which they are ignorant; yet if they knew about it, they could easily be cured.

THE HOLY SPIRIT REGENERATES THE SINNER

By applying the written Word, the Spirit of God creates in the sinner a new mind to believe and a new heart to love the truth of God.

> Unless one is born again, he cannot see the kingdom of God . . . unless one is born of water and the Spirit, he cannot enter the kingdom of God (John 3:3, 5 NKJV; see also vv. 6–8; compare Ephesians 5:26).

> Now if any man have not the Spirit of Christ, he is none of his (Romans 8:9).

In other words, the Holy Spirit does for the soul what the nurse does for the patient. There is medicine on the table that will make the sick man better, but how is he to get it? Someone must administer it. Here is a soul that is lost. Christ is the Savior, the Redeemer, of that soul. He purchased forgiveness, but how is the sinner to obtain it? "We are made partakers of," that is, we receive "the redemption purchased by Christ . . . by the effectual application of it to us by his Holy Spirit."

The moment the sinner is born again by the Spirit of God and the Word of God, he is baptized by the Holy Spirit and becomes a member of the body of Christ, the church. Therefore, the believer does not *seek* the baptism of the Spirit, for he has already received it.

> For by one Spirit we were all baptized into one body, whether Jews or Greeks, whether slaves or free; and have all been made to drink into one Spirit (1 Corinthians 12:13 NKJV).

Not only does the Holy Spirit regenerate the sinner at the moment be believes in Christ, and at the same moment baptize him into the body of Christ; but he also comes into him to indwell him forever (John 14:16–17) and seals him, thus indicating God's ownership and the believer's security (Ephesians 1:13).

The Holy Spirit is referred to by Paul as "the guarantee of our inheritance" (Ephesians 1:14 NKJV). The blessings of his presence within us are proof that there is more to come.

All of these ministries of the Holy Spirit—regeneration, baptism, indwelling, and sealing—are accomplished once and for all for the believer *when he believes.*

But it is tragically true that many who have been born again *quench* and *grieve* the Holy Spirit of God in a multitude of ways, even though we have been commanded to "be filled with the Spirit." To heed this command, we must walk with God, obey him, and claim his promise of power over Satan, which comes through Bible study, prayer, and love for him who "spared not his own Son, but freely gave him up for us all" (Romans 8:32).

THE HOLY SPIRIT INDWELLS THE BELIEVER AND EMPOWERS HIM FOR SERVICE

The indwelling of the Holy Spirit is permanent. The filling of the Spirit empowers the believer to live a Christlike life and at particular times to accomplish special service (see Acts 1:8). This ministry may be interrupted by sin in the believer's life. For this reason, the filling of the Spirit needs to be repeated.

We need to remember that our bodies are sacred because they are a dwelling place of God.

> "Or do you not know that your body is a temple of the Holy Spirit who is in you, whom you have from God, and that you are not your own? For you have been bought with a price: therefore glorify God in your body" (1 Corinthians 6:19–20, NASB).

The indwelling Holy Spirit is the believer's comforter, teacher, and guide.

> But the Helper, the Holy Spirit, whom the Father will send in my name, He will teach you all things, and bring to your remembrance all that I said to you (John 14:26 NASB, see also John 15:26; 16:12–15).

As our teacher, the Spirit of God enlightens our minds in the knowledge of Christ.

> Now we have received, not the spirit of the world, but the spirit which is of God; that we might know the things that are freely given to us of God (1 Corinthians 2:12).

There is a world of important spiritual truth that we

could neither understand nor enjoy were it not for the Holy Spirit working in us.

Moreover, he empowers us for service by renewing our wills.

> Not by works of righteousness which we have done, but according to His mercy He saved us, through the washing of regeneration and renewing of the Holy Spirit (Titus 3:5 NKJV).

> That he would grant you, according to the riches of his glory, to be strengthened with might by his Spirit in the inner man" (Ephesians 3:16).

It is one thing to know the truth, and it is another thing to *act* upon and *obey it.* If the Holy Spirit only enlightened our minds in the knowledge of Christ without moving upon our wills, if he only taught us the truth but did not make us disposed to believe and do it, then we should not be as well off, perhaps, as if we had been left in ignorance. But the gracious Spirit of God does not leave his work of mercy half done. He not only enlightens our minds, but he also renews our wills. He shows us the truth and he gives us the disposition to love it. We sometimes grow weary and faint in our minds. Then the Holy Spirit comes to our relief, strengthens our faith, encourages our hearts, and *empowers us to do the will of God.* Then we realize our utter dependence upon him and can say with the prophet of old:

> "Not by might nor by power, but by My Spirit," says the LORD of hosts (Zechariah 4:6).

10

What the Bible Says about Faith and Repentance

It is hopeless to depend on good works to earn eternal life. The Ten Commandments are like the ten links of a chain by which a person hangs suspended over a cliff. Only one link needs to be broken to result in death. Along this line, James wrote:

> Whosoever shall keep the whole law, and yet offend in one point, he is guilty of all (James 2:10).

For example, if you have coveted something that belongs

to someone else, you have broken the Ten Commandments. The condition for salvation taught in the Bible is not good works but faith.

> Believe on the Lord Jesus Christ, and you will be saved, you and your household (Acts 16:31 NKJV).

Some people speak of different "steps" that the sinner must take in order to come to salvation, and they sometimes cite passages of Scripture in which repentance is mentioned, as though it were a separate "step" in addition to faith. When the teaching of Scripture is properly presented and understood, faith and repentance are seen as inseparable; they are in reality "two sides of the same coin." That they are not two separate acts is proven by the gospel of John, which was written to show people how to be saved and which does not even mention repentance. If repentance were a separate act in addition to believing, then the instruction in John would be incomplete.

> But these are written that you may believe that Jesus is the Christ, the Son of God, and that believing you may have life in His name (John 20:31 NKJV).

Of course, all those who really do believe, as instructed in the Gospel of John, also repent; for saving faith includes repentance, just as genuine repentance includes saving faith.

Although faith and repentance cannot be separated in practice, we can make an artificial separation for the purpose of studying what they are.

FAITH

1. Faith is receiving Jesus Christ

In salvation we give nothing; we receive everything. Our hearts are corrupt and therefore unacceptable to God. They must be cleansed from sin before they can become a proper offering to him. But this cleansing is brought about only through the blood of Jesus, which is applied to us by faith.

> But as many as received him, to them gave he power to become the sons of God, even to them that believe on his name (John 1:12).

> But if we walk in the light, as he is in the light, we have fellowship one with another, and the blood of Jesus Christ his Son [cleanses] us from all sin (1 John 1:7).

2. Faith is receiving and resting upon Jesus Christ

To rest upon Christ means to no longer be anxious about the result. He who has true faith in Christ has no doubt that his sins are all forgiven and that he is truly and eternally reconciled to God. Therefore, his soul is at peace on these matters.

> You will keep him in perfect peace, whose mind is stayed on You, because he trusts in You (Isaiah 26:3 NKJV).

3. Faith is receiving and resting upon Jesus Christ alone

The person who trusts partly in God and partly in himself does not show true faith in Jesus Christ. God does not permit any partnership in the work of salvation. All the work we do will never save us from sin. Good works should follow salvation, but our works cannot take the place of our Savior. He stands alone as our redeemer.

> But we are all as an unclean thing, and all our righteousnesses are as filthy rags; and we all do fade as a leaf; and our iniquities, like the wind, have taken us away (Isaiah 64:6).

> For by grace are [you] saved through faith; and that not of yourselves: it is the gift of God: not of works, lest any man should boast (Ephesians 2:8–9).

Someone has defined faith by using each letter of the word to begin a word: Forsaking All I Take Him.

> Not by works of righteousness which we have done, but according to His mercy He saved us, through the washing of regeneration and renewing of the Holy Spirit (Titus 3:5 NKJV).

4. *Faith is receiving and resting upon Jesus Christ alone as he is offered to us in the gospel*

Our own fancies about Christ are not enough. We have no authority for trusting in human ideas about Christ. We must know what kind of Savior Christ is. This we can learn only in the Bible, which tells us clearly who the Lord Jesus Christ is and what he has done for us.

> And he said unto them, These are the words which I [spoke] unto you, while I was yet with you, that all things must be fulfilled, which were written in the law of Moses, and in the prophets, and in the psalms, concerning me (Luke 24:44).

> This is a faithful saying, and worthy of all acceptation, that Christ Jesus came into the world to save sinners (1 Timothy 1:15).

> Christ died for our sins according to the scriptures . . . he was buried, and . . . he rose again the third day according to the scriptures (1 Corinthians 15:3–4).

> . . . being justified freely by his grace through the redemption that is in Christ Jesus: whom God [has] set forth to be a propitiation through faith in his blood, to declare his righteousness for the remission of sins that are past, through the forbearance of God (Romans 3:24–25).

Whether this decision is made during a public meeting or while alone, it should be made known to others in some way (Matthew 10:32).

REPENTANCE

1. The necessity for repentance

To prove the importance of repentance, Jesus said:

> I tell you, no; but unless you repent you will all likewise perish (Luke 13:3 NKJV).

> "Thus it is written, and thus it was necessary for the Christ to suffer and to rise from the dead the third day and that repentance and remission of sins should be preached in His name to all nations" (Luke 24:46–47).

John the Baptist had preached, saying, "Repent, for the kingdom of heaven is at hand!" (Matthew 3:2 NKJV). Christ reiterated the same message (Matthew 4:17). And the

apostles "went out, and preached that men should repent" (Mark 6:12). The following are some of their inspired words concerning the necessity for repentance:

> Repent therefore and be converted, that your sins
> may be blotted out, so that times of refreshing may
> come from the presence of the Lord (Acts 3:19 NKJV).

> Truly, these times of ignorance God overlooked, but
> now commands all men everywhere to repent (Acts
> 17:30 NKJV).

> The Lord is . . . not willing that any should perish, but
> that all should come to repentance (2 Peter 3:9).

We have seen that the only thing necessary to salvation
is faith in the finished work of the Lord Jesus Christ. Those
who thus receive Christ will repent of their sins.

2. Repentance—a change of mind toward God

The word *repentance* means "a change of mind" or
purpose. It is well illustrated by the publican (Luke 18:13);
by the prodigal son (Luke 15:17–21); and by the son who
first refused to obey his father's command to work in his
vineyard, "but afterward . . . repented, and went" (Matthew 21:29). Repentance is, therefore, a turning away
from sin—a definite "change of mind" toward God as a
result of genuine heart conviction of sin. Paul preached
to Jew and Gentile, saying "that they should repent, turn
to God, and do works befitting repentance" (Acts 26:20).
Isaiah sounded the warning:

> Let the wicked forsake his way, and the unrighteous
> man his thoughts: and let him return unto the LORD,

and he will have mercy upon him; and to our God,
for he will abundantly pardon (Isaiah 55:7).

Some think that repentance is the same as sorrow for
sin, but this is by no means true. Sorrow for sin in itself is
not repentance, but "godly sorrow produces repentance
leading to salvation" (2 Corinthians 7:10 NKJV). One may
be sorry for sin just because of the trouble into which it
gets him, or because of the grief and loss it brings upon
him, without ever thinking of the dishonor it brings to
God. A child will say "I'm sorry" to escape punishment.
But if he is not truly repentant he will commit the same
misdeed again. This is merely a form of the "sorrow of the
world" that "produces death" (2 Corinthians 7:10 NKJV).
One who is truly sorry for sin because he knows it is an
abominable thing that God hates will turn away from sin
unto God—that is repentance.

Thus far we have been thinking of repentance in the
life of an unsaved person who turns to Jesus Christ for
salvation. Only as we see ourselves as guilty sinners before
God do we acknowledge our need of a Savior, upon whom
the Lord has laid the iniquity of us all (Isaiah 53:6).

But let us think now of the believer's attitude toward
God when, after he has been saved, he falls into sin. Satan
does not leave the redeemed of the Lord alone, and his
attacks are both subtle and ceaselessly active. While the
believer's eternal security is not in question (John
10:27–30), it is his solemn responsibility to be more than
conqueror over Satan through Christ Jesus (Romans 8:37)
by the power of the indwelling Holy Spirit (Romans 8;
Ephesians 5:18; Galatians 5:16). If, in a moment of weak-
ness, the Christian does fall into sin, he should immediately confess it and forsake it. He should name the sin

before God at the moment he is aware he has committed it. Confession to another person is not necessary unless that other person is aware that you have injured him in some way.

The New Testament epistles are filled with exhortation and instruction concerning the confession and forgiveness of sin in the believer's life. One passage, written to Christians, which sums up the whole matter is the following:

> If we confess our sins, He is faithful and just to forgive us our sins and to cleanse us from all unrighteousness. . . . My little children, these things I write to you, so that you may not sin. And if anyone sins, we have an Advocate with the Father, Jesus Christ the righteous. And He Himself is the propitiation for our sins, and not for ours only but also for the whole world (1 John 1:9; 2:1–2 NKJV).

If one truly loves the Lord, he will be sorry for his sin because it offends God—so very sorry for it that he will not intend to commit it again. Moreover, he will seek to live so close to his Savior that all known sin—not just particular disobedience—will be confessed instantly and as quickly pardoned by the God of forgiving love. He can do this only by the power of the indwelling Christ.

> For I know that in me (that is, in my flesh) nothing good dwells; for to will is present with me, but how to perform what is good I do not find (Romans 7:18 NKJV ; compare vv. 15–25).

> I can do all things through Christ who strengthens me (Philippians 4:13 NKJV).

But how are we to know what sin is, and thus be led to

repent? This question too is answered in the Scriptures, which say that conviction comes from the Holy Spirit.

3. Repentance—the work of the Holy Spirit in the sinner's heart

It is the work of the Holy Spirit to make us see that we are sinners. Before he went to the cross, the Lord Jesus said to the eleven who loved him:

> Nevertheless I tell you the truth: It is expedient for you that I go away: for if I go not away, the Comforter will not come unto you; but if I depart, I will send him unto you. And when he is come, he will reprove the world of sin, and of righteousness, and of judgment (John 16:7–8).

The word *reprove* in this sentence means to "convince." The Holy Spirit speaks to us through the Bible, which he wrote, to show us the things of Christ (see John 15:26; 16:12–15; compare John 3:5–8 with Ephesians 5:26).

There may be some believers who cannot remember the exact moment of their conversion, but they are an exception. The experience of salvation is like the commitment made by a young couple when they become engaged. Their later marriage ceremony before friends and relatives is like the believer's public confession of Christ.

> For with the heart one believes unto righteousness, and with the mouth confession is made unto salvation (Romans 10:10 NKJV).

11

What the Bible Says about a Believer's Heritage

When God forgives our sins they are taken away forever. In addition God gives the believer his immeasurable riches—both now and in the future life.

IN THIS LIFE

The blessings that come from our union with Christ may be summarized in three words: *justification, adoption,* and *sanctification.*

1. Justification

And by Him everyone who believes is justified from all things from which you could not be justified by the law of Moses (Acts 13:39 NKJV).

The Bible teaches that justification is the act of God whereby he declares the sinner to be righteous through faith in Jesus Christ. A righteous God must have a righteous basis for such a declaration, and his righteous basis is the death of the Lord Jesus.

He [God] made him who knew no sin to be sin on our behalf, that we might become the righteousness of God in Him (2 Corinthians 5:21 NASB).

We are said to be "justified . . . by his grace" (Romans 3:24); "justified by his blood" (Romans 5:9); and "justified by faith" (Romans 3:28; 5:1). These expressions teach that God's grace is the source of justification; Christ's death is the basis of it; and faith is the channel through which it is received.

The believing sinner is declared righteous in God's sight because through faith he is identified with Christ and shares the benefits of his death. Not only are his sins forgiven, but God graciously looks upon him as though he had not sinned; indeed, he sees him "in Christ," with Christ's positive righteousness reckoned to him. He is accounted righteous, not through any righteousness of his own, but through Christ's righteousness which covers him.

2. Adoption

In ordinary usage adoption is the act of making another person's child one's own. The word *adoption* is used five times in the English Bible. One of these occurrences refers to the completion of our redemption in the resurrection of the body (Romans 8:23); another refers to Israel's favored position in Old Testament times (Romans 9:4). The other three have to do with the believer's position now.

> For you did not receive the spirit of bondage again to fear, but you received the Spirit of adoption by whom we cry out, "Abba, Father" (Romans 8:15 NKJV).

> Having predestinated us unto the adoption of children by Jesus Christ to himself, according to the good pleasure of his will" (Ephesians 1:5).

> But when the fullness of the time had come, God sent forth His Son, born of a woman, born under the law, to redeem those who were under the law, that we might receive the adoption as sons. And because you are sons, God has sent forth the Spirit of His Son into your hearts, crying out, "Abba, Father!" Therefore you are no longer a slave but a son, and if a son, then an heir of God through Christ (Galatians 4:4–7 NKJV).

These passages indicate that the scriptural doctrine of adoption involves much more than the customary usage of the word. The word that is translated as *adoption* means "to place as a son." The question often is raised: If we are born into the family of God, why do we need to be adopted? The answer is this: we are *children* of God by the new birth, *sons* of God by adoption. Through regeneration, or the new birth, we enter God's family (John 1:12–13, NASB); this is a matter of relationship. But adoption has to do with our position in God's family, not with our relationship. Galatians 3–4 explains the whole point of this doctrine of adoption—that every believer is an *adult child* in God's family. Although many believers, in their experience, are "babes in Christ" (1 Corinthians 3:1), in their standing, they are full-grown sons, with all the privileges of sonship.

> For you are all sons of God through faith in Christ Jesus (Galatians 3:26).

Regeneration and adoption take place at the same time. At the moment one believes he becomes a child of God, and at the same moment be becomes an adult son.

3. *Sanctification*

In each of the original languages in which the Bible was written (the Old Testament in Hebrew and the New Testament in Greek), the word that is translated *sanctify* has as its root meaning "to set apart. " It can even be used in the worship of God (see Exodus 30:26–29).

The words that are translated in the English Bible as *sanctify, sanctification, saint, holy,* and *holiness* are all related to one another in meaning. When God sanctifies a person, he sets that person apart unto himself; this involves, of course, the truth that the person is set apart from sin. There are three aspects of our sanctification.

a. *Positional sanctification*

> By that will we have been sanctified through the offering of the body of Jesus Christ once for all (Hebrews 10:10 NKJV).

The moment a person is united to Christ by faith, God sets him apart from the world.

> But know that the LORD [has] set apart him that is
> godly for himself: the LORD will hear when I call unto
> him (Psalm 4:3).

In their position or standing before God all believers have been sanctified. We can see this in the case of the Corinthian Christians, who are addressed as "sanctified in Christ Jesus, called to be saints" (1 Corinthians 1:2), even though their lives were far from what God wanted them to be. In other words, while a Christian may not always act like God's child, he still is one.

b. *Experiential, or practical, sanctification.* In their experience believers are being sanctified. This is a process by which the Holy Spirit is conforming them more and more to the likeness of Jesus Christ. Our positional sanctification ought to inspire us to seek practical sanctification. There are at least two conditions a believer must meet to open the way for the Holy Spirit's work in his life.

YIELDEDNESS TO GOD

> I beseech you therefore, brethren, by the mercies of
> God, that you present your bodies a living sacrifice,
> holy, acceptable to God, which is your reasonable
> service. And do not be conformed to this world, but
> be transformed by the renewing of your mind, that
> you may prove what is that good and acceptable and
> perfect will of God (Romans 12:1–2 NKJV).

Only as we yield ourselves to God, giving ourselves over to him completely, can the Holy Spirit produce his fruit in our lives (Galatians 5:16–25). It is possible to be a Christian without being yielded to God, but it is not possible to be a Spirit-filled Christian without surrender.

And do not present your members as instruments of unrighteousness to sin, but present yourselves to God as being alive from the dead, and your members as instruments of righteousness to God (Romans 6:13 NKJV).

FAITH

The believer must depend on the Holy Spirit moment by moment for victory over temptation. He must believe that Christ can and will live his life through him. Paul testified:

I have been crucified with Christ; it is no longer I who live, but Christ lives in me; and the life which I now live in the flesh I live by faith in the Son of God, who loved me and gave Himself for me (Galatians 2:20 NKJV).

c. *Ultimate sanctification.* Believers will be entirely sanctified at the return of the Lord Jesus Christ. (See 1 Thessalonians 5:23.) Then our experience will be in perfect harmony with our position. This is a future, rather than a present, benefit. This is shown by John's advice to believers:

My little children, these things I write to you, so that you may not sin. And if anyone sins, we have an Advocate with the Father, Jesus Christ the righteous (1 John 2:1 NKJV).

When we realize that God has forgiven our sins and put his own righteousness upon us, that he has made us his children with all the privileges of sonship, and that he has set us apart for himself and is causing us to grow in grace, how can we doubt his love for us? And if we cannot doubt his love for us, what hinders our having perfect peace and joy in our hearts all the time? If he thus loves us, can we keep from loving him in return? If we love him, shall we not obey him? And if we obey him, shall we not desire to be transformed into his "image from glory to glory, just as from the Lord the Spirit" (2 Corinthians 3:18 NASB).

> Having therefore these promises, dearly beloved, let us cleanse ourselves from all filthiness of the flesh and spirit, perfecting holiness in the fear of God (2 Corinthians 7:1).

4. *Assurance*

While it is possible for a true Christian to doubt his salvation, the result of justification, adoption, and sanctification is a growing assurance that we have truly been saved.

A child develops an assurance of belonging to his family by reading what is written on his birth certificate, by noting his resemblance to his parents, and by listening to them tell him he is their child. In the same way a Christian's assurance is based on what is written in God's Word (1 John 5:13), his growing likeness to Christ (1 John 3:10), and the witness of the Spirit telling him he is God's child (Romans 8:15–16).

5. *Security*

Once a person is saved God is able to keep him from losing that salvation.

> Unto him that is able to keep you from falling, and to present you faultless before the presence of his glory (Jude 24).

Christ promised that his sheep would never perish but have eternal life (John 10:27–28).

> Therefore He is also able to save to the uttermost those who come to God through Him, since He always lives to make intercession for them (Hebrews 7:25 NKJV).

IN THE LIFE TO COME

1. The sting of death removed

The believer does not fear death because its sting has been removed by Christ in his death and resurrection.

> Forasmuch then as the children are partakers of flesh and blood, he also himself likewise took part of the same; that through death he might destroy him that had the power of death, that is, the devil; and deliver them who through fear of death were all their lifetime subject to bondage (Hebrews 2:14–15).

> O death, where is thy sting? O grave, where is thy victory? The sting of death is sin; and the strength of sin is the law. But thanks be to God, which [gives] us the victory through our Lord Jesus Christ (1 Corinthians 15:55–57; see also 2 Corinthians 5:1–2).

2. "Absent from the body . . . present with the Lord" (2 Corinthians 5:8)

At death the spirits of believers go to be with Christ, even as he said to the penitent thief on the cross:

> And Jesus said to him, "Assuredly, I say to you, today you will be with Me in Paradise" (Luke 23:43 NKJV).

Paul expressed this same truth, not only in 2 Corinthians 5:8, but also in Philippians 1:23 NKJV:

> For I am hard pressed between the two, having a desire to depart and be with Christ, which is far better.

While the spirits of the redeemed are with Christ, their bodies rest in the grave until the first resurrection (1 Thessalonians 4:13–18; Revelation 20:4–6).

3. To be "raised in glory" (1 Corinthians 15:43)

When the Lord Jesus Christ comes again, he will bring forth the spirits of believers with him and will call forth their bodies from the grave. Then they will live forever, completely redeemed, in glorified, resurrected bodies.

a. *"We shall be like him"* (1 John 3:2). God's purpose of conforming us to the image of his Son will be perfectly fulfilled (Romans 8:29).

> For our citizenship is in heaven, from which also we eagerly wait for a Savior, the Lord Jesus Christ; who will transform the body of our humble state into conformity with the body of his glory, by the exertion of the power that he has even to subject all things to Himself (Philippians 3:20–21 NASB).

b. *Our resurrection bodies will be real.* The glorified bodies of believers will be like Christ's, and his risen body was real—a body of "flesh and bones" (Luke 24:39). First Corinthians 15 is the central passage on the resurrection, showing us that we will be the same, yet not the same—the same in individual identity, yet changed in constituent particles and appearance.

c. *We shall know the fullness of blessing—in spirit, soul, and body.*

> And God shall wipe away all tears from their eyes; and there shall be no more death, neither sorrow, nor crying, neither shall there be any more pain: for the former things are passed away (Revelation 21:4).

d. *We shall be "to the praise of his glory"* (Ephesians 1:12; 3:10–11).

> That he might present it to himself a glorious church, not having spot, or wrinkle, or any such thing; but that it should be holy and without blemish (Ephesians 5:27).

The purity of heaven will not admit of the presence of anything that is sinful or defiling.

> But there shall by no means enter it anything that defiles, or causes an abomination or a lie, but only those who are written in the Lamb's Book of Life (Revelation 21:27 NKJV).

The blessing to come to believers can be summed up in the full enjoyment of God himself forever and ever.

Try to imagine life where the very thought of an eventual end to things is taken away, where life will simply go on and on. Add to that the prospect of being engaged in the blissful occupation of serving God in his presence throughout all eternity!

> His servants shall serve him: and they shall see his face (Revelation 22:3–4).

The psalmist said it well:

> You will show me the path of life; in Your presence is fullness of joy; at Your right hand are pleasures forevermore (Psalm 16:11 NKJV).

12

What the Bible Says about the Christian Life

Everyone who has accepted the Lord Jesus Christ as personal Savior ought to grow in his Christian experience. He could not *grow into* the Christian life, but had to be *born into* it by a spiritual birth. Nevertheless, once in this life by God's grace through faith in Christ, he can and should grow in it. We have seen previously that in position every believer is, from the moment he believes, an adult son of God. In his Christian experience, however, every believer starts as a spiritual baby.

In the previous chapter, we noted that the growth in grace commanded by Scripture (2 Peter 3:18) is an element of sanctification. Now we want to consider some of the means God uses to bring about our spiritual growth.

God has given us certain helps—sometimes referred to as the means of grace—that we may know him better, overcome the power of sin in our lives, and become more and more like him. Why is it that some Christians never grow, or make so little progress in their spiritual experience? Because they neglect the means of growth that God has appointed. Read in this connection 1 Corinthians 3:1–4 and Hebrews 5:11–14.

There are four basic requirements for spiritual growth: (1) the study and application of the Word of God; (2) the practice of prayer; (3) the assembling of ourselves together; and (4) the God-given ordinances.

THE STUDY OF THE WORD OF GOD

Of first importance among the God-given helps to Christian growth is his own inspired Word.

> As newborn babes, desire the pure milk of the word, that you may grow thereby (1 Peter 2:2 NKJV).

In the everyday affairs of life we know that we cannot master any subject without careful study; yet many Christians imagine that God in some mysterious way will give them spiritual knowledge without their needing to study the Bible. Here are some suggestions of ways in which we should study God's Word.

1. We should study the Word with diligence

The people of Berea who heard the preaching of Paul

are an example of those who search the Bible regularly and diligently.

> These were more noble than those in Thessalonica, in that they received the word with all readiness of mind, and searched the scriptures daily, whether those things were so (Acts 17:11).

Unless we do as much as this, the study will not be very honoring to God or very helpful to us.

> Be diligent to present yourself approved to God as a workman who does not need to be ashamed, handling accurately the word of truth (2 Timothy 2:15 NASB).

2. *We should study the Bible with humility of spirit*

We are taught to receive the Word with meekness.

> Therefore lay aside all filthiness and overflow of wickedness, and receive with meekness the implanted word, which is able to save your souls (James 1:21).

We must not be too proud to learn or to obey what we read. When we come to something in the Word that is beyond our understanding, we must purpose to believe it anyway. We also must resolve to obey God's Word, even though such obedience may be difficult at times.

3. *We should study the Bible prayerfully*

We need the help of God to make us understand his Word as we read it.

> Open my eyes, that I may see wondrous things from Your law (Psalm 119:18 NKJV).

The reason many persons say they do not understand the Scriptures, and hence are not interested in reading them, is that they do not ask God to be their teacher.

He opened their understanding, that they might comprehend the Scriptures (Luke 24:45 NKJV; see also 24:25–32).

But the Helper, the Holy Spirit, whom the Father will send in My name, He will teach you all things, and bring to your remembrance all things that I said to you (John 14:26 NKJV; see also 15:26; 16:12–15).

4. We should study the Word with appreciation of its value

For centuries, the only Bible available to many believers was chained to a desk in the village church. Frequently Christians had to pay for the privilege of having a Bible to read for even a short time. Even today many Christians in some parts of the world have little or no access to a Bible. Let us never forget what a valuable possession the Bible is. The psalmist said:

The fear of the LORD is clean, enduring forever: the judgments of the LORD are true and righteous altogether. More to be desired are they than gold, yea, than much fine gold (Psalm 19:9–10 NKJV).

THE PRACTICE OF PRAYER

The second basic requirement is maintaining a consistent prayer life. Let us consider what prayer is.

1. *Prayer is the soul's adoration of God*

Adoration is worship. Following are a few of the numerous similar passages of Scripture that express adoration of God:

> And Hannah prayed and said: "My heart rejoices in the LORD; my horn is exalted in the LORD. I smile at my enemies, because I rejoice in Your salvation. No one is holy like the LORD, for there is none besides You, nor is there any rock like our God (1 Samuel 2:1–2 NKJV).

> Therefore You are great, O Lord GOD. For there is none like You, nor is there any God besides You, according to all that we have heard with our ears (2 Samuel 7:22 NKJV).

> Great is the LORD, and greatly to be praised; and his greatness is unsearchable (Psalm 145:3).

In these instances the persons who pray do not make any requests of God at all; they do not even praise or thank him especially for what he has done; but they just speak in rapture of his salvation, his holiness, his power, his greatness, his wonderful goodness. Their souls are taken up entirely with the thought of him, of what he is in himself. This is adoration, and this is one form or one part of prayer.

2. *Prayer is the expression of our desires before God*

Thus it is something more than adoration. It is telling God what we think we need, and what we wish he would give us. Jacob asked him for food and clothing (Genesis

28:20), and so may we; but there are some things far more important than these for which to ask him. Our spiritual needs far outweigh our material needs, and we ought to recognize this fact in our praying as Paul did in his (Ephesians 1:15–23).

> If then you were raised with Christ, seek those things which are above, where Christ is, sitting at the right hand of God (Colossians 3:1 NKJV).

3. *Prayer is asking God for things that are in accord with his will*

We cannot expect God to give us things that are not best for us. The reason some of our prayers are not answered is because we ask for such things.

> You ask and do not receive, because you ask amiss, that you may spend it on your pleasures (James 4:3 NKJV).

If we trust only in our own judgment we cannot expect to know God's will for us. But he has told us much about his will in his written Word, and he has given us the Holy Spirit to help us. Therefore, when we ask for the guidance of the Holy Spirit, we may have confidence that we are praying according to his will.

> And in the same way the Spirit also helps our weaknesses; for we do not know how to pray as we should, but the Spirit himself intercedes for us with groanings too deep for words; and he who searches the hearts knows what the mind of the Spirit is, because He intercedes for the saints according to the will of God (Romans 8:26–27 NASB).

And this is the confidence that we have in him, that, if we ask any thing according to his will, he [hears] us (1 John 5:14).

4. *Prayer is petitioning the Father in the name of his Son, Jesus Christ, our Savior*

Because we are so sinful, we have no possible claim on God; we have no right to come into his presence for anything. Everything depends upon the redemptive work of Christ. It is he who intercedes for us.

> Therefore He is also able to save to the uttermost those who come to God through Him, since He always lives to make intercession for them (Hebrews 7:25 NKJV).

> And whatever you ask in My name, that I will do, that the Father may be glorified in the Son (John 14:13 NKJV; see also 14:14; 15:16; 16:23–24).

5. *Prayer includes the confession of sin*

We should be careful not to omit confession, for we always stand in need of it, and it helps to keep us humble and grateful before God. Read Luke 18:9–14.

> If I regard iniquity in my heart, the Lord will not hear me (Psalm 66:18).

> If we confess our sins, he is faithful and just to forgive us our sins, and to cleanse us from all unrighteousness (1 John 1:9).

6. *Prayer is linked with the thankful acknowledgement of God's mercies*

It is selfish always to be asking God for blessings and

never thanking him for those already received. Such a thankless soul cannot expect much from God not because he demands the pay of our gratitude for what he does, but because the man who does not feel grateful is one whom it would not be well to gratify.

> Bless the LORD, O my soul, and forget not all his benefits (Psalm 103:2).

> Be anxious for nothing, but in everything by prayer and supplication with thanksgiving let your requests be made known to God (Philippians 4:6 NASB).

7. Effectual prayer is persevering— the expression of faith

Read Luke 11:5–13; 18:1–8 for illustrations of the truth expressed in the following passages:

> So Jesus said to them, "Because of your unbelief; for assuredly, I say to you, if you have faith as a mustard seed, you will say to this mountain, 'Move from here to there,' and it will move; and nothing will be impossible for you" (Matthew 17:20 NKJV).

> And whatever things you ask in prayer, believing, you will receive (Matthew 21:22 NKJV; see also 1 John 5:14–15).

> The effective, fervent prayer of a righteous man avails much (James 5:16 NKJV).

THE ASSEMBLING OF OURSELVES TOGETHER

The third basic requirement for consistent Christian growth is fellowship with other believers. Attending church, engaging in the public worship of God, and listening to the preaching of the gospel—these things not only edify believers and help them grow in grace, they also are a means of testifying for Christ before sinners and saints.

> Not forsaking the assembling of ourselves together, as is the manner of some, but exhorting one another, and so much the more as you see the Day approaching (Hebrews 10:25 NKJV).

GOD-GIVEN ORDINANCES

The fourth basic requirement for spiritual growth is the observance of the God-given ordinances (or outward signs). Baptism and the Lord's Supper are the two ordinances by which we are known as Christ's people and by which we may grow in grace.

> "Can anyone forbid water, that these should not be baptized who have received the Holy Spirit just as we have?" And he commanded them to be baptized in the name of the Lord. Then they asked him to stay a few days (Acts 10:47–48 NKJV).

> And he took bread, and gave thanks, and brake it, and gave unto them, saying, "This is my body which is given for you: this do in rememberance of me." Likewise also the cup after supper, saying, "This cup is the new testament in my blood, which is shed for you" (Luke 22:19–20).

Many people go to the Lord's table who are not truly converted. They may even have been baptized but are not born again. All who are truly converted are expected to obey our Lord's command by being baptized and by participating in the Lord's Supper. Something is very wrong with them if they do not heed his Word in these things.

1. What is baptism?

Baptism is the symbolic use of water in the name of the Father, and of the Son, and of the Holy Spirit.

> Go therefore and make disciples of all the nations, baptizing them in the name of the Father and of the Son and of the Holy Spirit (Matthew 28:19 NKJV).

Baptism was commanded by Christ to express outwardly the inner work of the Spirit. Baptism symbolizes this work but is not, and never can be, a substitute for it. Baptism cannot save the soul. A sinner is regenerated only by the Holy Spirit who applies the Word of God to the heart and makes the guilty soul a "new creation" in Christ Jesus (2 Corinthians 5:17; John 3: 3–8, 16). At the same time that he regenerates the believing sinner, the Holy Spirit puts him into the body of Christ. This, and this only, is the baptism by the Spirit "into one body" (1 Corinthians 12:13), of which water baptism is a symbol.

2. What is the Lord's Supper?

a. *The Lord's Supper is a memorial of our redemption by Christ's death.* The Lord's Supper helps us remember our Savior's death on the cross for us— until he comes. When he appears in glory, we will not need to remember him; for we will dwell in his presence forevermore!

> This do in remembrance of me (Luke 22:19).

> For as often as you eat this bread and drink this cup,

you proclaim the Lord's death till he comes (1 Corinthians 11:26).

b. *The Lord's Supper is a sign of the fellowship that we have with Christ and with our fellow believers in him.* People who sit down and eat together at the same table are supposed to be friends. When we gather around the Lord's table, we show to the world that we are one—not only with Christ but also with one another. For this reason the Scripture speaks of the Lord's Supper as the Communion.

> The cup of blessing which we bless, is it not the communion of the blood of Christ? The bread which we break, is it not the communion of the body of Christ? For we being many are one bread, and one body: for we are all partakers of that one bread (1 Corinthians 10:16–17).

Since the Lord's Supper is a memorial and a sign, we do not literally eat the body and drink the blood of Christ. The elements represent his body and blood symbolically. We feed on him by faith, to gather spiritual strength from day to day, as he said in John 6:30–58.

We are warned against partaking of the Lord's Supper "unworthily." It is required that we have knowledge and appreciation of the Lord's atoning death and faith in him as our own Savior to participate in this sacred ordinance in a worthy manner. We must trust in him alone for redemption. Moreover, we should examine our own hearts, as we are commanded to do, before participating in the Lord's Supper. This implies confession of sin and God's forgiveness.

> Let a man examine himself, and so let him eat of that

bread, and drink of that cup (1 Corinthians 11:28; see also vv. 20–34).

As we let the Holy Spirit apply to our hearts the truth to be learned from these four ways of growing in grace—the Word of God, prayer, the assembling of ourselves together, and the God-given ordinances—we will not be conformed to this world, but will be transformed by the renewing of our minds, that we may prove what is that good, and acceptable, and perfect, will of God (see Romans 12:2).

Then at life's end we will be able to say with Paul:

I have fought a good fight, I have finished the race, I have kept the faith. Finally, there is laid up for me the crown of righteousness, which the Lord, the righteous Judge, will give to me on that Day (2 Timothy 4:7–8 NKJV).

As Dwight L. Moody lay dying, he looked up toward heaven and said, "Earth is receding, heaven is opening, this is my coronation day!"

May such a coronation day await you in glory.

Bibliography

For those who want to do further study, the books listed below are particularly valuable.

Chafer, Lewis Sperry and John F. Walvoord. *Major Bible Themes*. Grand Rapids, Mich.: Zondervan Publishing House.

Day, Millard F. *Basic Bible Doctrines*. Chicago: Moody Press.

Evans, William. *Great Doctrines of the Bible*. Chicago: Moody Press.

Ironside, Harry A. *Sailing with Paul: Simple Papers for Young Christians*. New York: Loizeaux Brothers.

Torrey, R. A. *What the Bible Teaches*. Westwood, N. J.: Revell Publishing Company.

What Christians Believe. Chicago: Moody Press.

Revelation 20:14–15
JUDGMENT OF THE UNSAVED
Chapter 5

Genesis 1:1
GOD THE CREATOR
Chapter 4

Hebrews 13:8
GOD NEVER CHANGES
Chapter 2

Revelation 4:11
PURPOSE OF CREATION
Chapter 5

2 Corinthians 13:14
TRINITY OF THE GODHEAD
Chapter 3

John 1:12
SALVATION
Chapter 2

John 1:3
GOD THE CREATOR
Chapter 4

Hebrews 11:1
DEFINITION OF FAITH
Chapter 3

2 Peter 1:21
INSPIRATION OF SCRIPTURE

Jesus Christ the same yesterday, and today, and forever.

In the beginning God created the heaven and the earth.

And death and hell were cast into the lake of fire. This is the second death

But as many as received him, to them gave he power to become the sons of God, even to them that believe on his name.

The grace of the Lord Jesus Christ, and the love of God, and the communion of the Holy Spirit, be with you all. Amen.

Thou art worthy, O Lord, to receive glory and honor and power: for thou hast created all things, and for thy pleasure they are and were created.

For the prophecy came not in old time by the will of man: but holy men of God spake as they were moved by the Holy Ghost.

Now faith is the substance of things hoped for, the evidence of things not seen.

All things were made by him: and without him was not anything made that was made.

Romans 5:1–2
JUSTIFICATION BY FAITH
Chapter 11

1 Corinthians 12:13
BAPTISM OF THE HOLY SPIRIT
Chapter 9

Matthew 28:20
OMNIPRESENCE OF CHRIST
Chapter 7

Titus 3:5
GOD'S MERCY IN SALVATION
Chapter 10

Hebrews 4:15
OUR GREAT HIGH PRIEST
Chapter 8

Matthew 28:18
OMNIPOTENCE OF CHRIST
Chapter 7

Ephesians 1:13
SEALING OF THE HOLY SPIRIT
Chapter 9

2 Corinthians 8:9
POVERTY OF CHRIST
Chapter 8

Romans 6:23
SIN'S WAGES
Chapter 6

Teaching them to observe all things whatsoever I have commanded you: and, lo, I am with you alway, even unto the end of the world. Amen.

For by one Spirit are we all baptized into one body, whether we be Jews or Gentiles, whether we be bond or free; and have been all made to drink into one Spirit.

Therefore being justified by faith, we have peace with God through our Lord Jesus Christ: By whom also we have access by faith into this grace wherein we stand, and rejoice in hope of the glory of God.

And Jesus came and spake unto them, saying, All power is given unto me in heaven and in earth.

For we have not an high priest which cannot be touched with the feeling of our infirmities, but was in all points tempted like as we are, yet without sin.

Not by works of righteousness which we have done, but according to his mercy he saved us, by the washing of regeneration, and renewing of the Holy Ghost.

For the wages of sin is death; but the gift of God is eternal life through Jesus Christ our Lord.

For ye know the grace of our Lord Jesus Christ, that, though he was rich, yet for your sakes he became poor, that ye through his poverty might be rich.

In whom ye also trusted, after that ye heard the word of truth, the gospel of your salvation, in whom also after that ye believed, ye were sealed with that Holy Spirit of promise.

1 John 5:14
EFFECTIVE PRAYER
Chapter 12

Psalm 119:18
A DEVOTIONAL PRAYER
Chapter 12

And this is the confidence that we have in him, that, if we ask anything according to his will, he heareth us.

Open thou mine eyes, that I may behold wondrous things out of thy law.